JAZZ

LEGENDS

Chick and Bunny Crumpacker

d Tom Kraus.

First edition
97   96   95   5   4   3   2   1

This is a Peregrine Smith Book, published by
Gibbs Smith, Publisher
P.O. Box 667
Layton, Utah 84041

Design by Randall Smith Associates
Edited by Gail Yngve

Cover illustration: Front cover photograph of John Coltrane by Raeburn Flerlage

Printed and bound in Singapore

Library of Congress Cataloging-in-Publication Data

Crumpacker, Bunny
Jazz Legends / Bunny and Chick Crumpacker.
     p.   cm.
ISBN 0-87905-683-5 (alk. paper)
    1. Jazz musicians—United States—Biography.
    2. Jazz—History and criticism. I. Title
ML385.C75 1995
781.65'092'2—dc20
[B]   95-21612
CIP   MN

JAZZ

LEGENDS

CONTENTS

INTRO-DUCTION

JAZZ, like so many other things worth knowing, is full of mystery and paradox. It's known as America's only native art form, which ignores the paintings, stories, music, and imagery of Native Americans. It also ignores the fact that jazz is, in many ways, a foreign art form. It was based on African traditions brought to our country by men and women stolen from their native continent to supply labor in the New World.

Jazz is called the music of the people. It is said to have begun in barrooms, brothels, Chicago speakeasies, New Orleans street bands, and Harlem rent parties. But many jazz artists came from well-to-do, well-educated families, and their mothers and fathers wouldn't have been caught dead at a rent party. They preferred debutante clubs and church organs.

Jazz is democratic, but

consider its aristocrats: King Oliver, Count Basie, Duke Ellington, Earl Hines, the King of Swing, and the Queen of Scat.

THE roots of jazz are black, but it has repeatedly been taken over by white musicians, white record producers, white disc jockeys, and, finally, white audiences. Each time jazz evolved into something new, with a different—and black—sound, it was discovered again by white musicians, white record producers, white disc jockeys, and, finally, white audiences. In this way, jazz evolved from spirituals, work songs, and gospel to ragtime and the blues, through Dixieland (Dixie), swing, bebop, and progressive jazz into fusion, rock and roll, and rap, with rhythm and blues and now zydeco along the way.

JAZZ is pure and easy, but its critics take the music apart, note by note, phrase by phrase, riff by riff, and then have enormous trouble putting it back together again.

Finally, no matter what its roots and genetics, jazz was born in America, but it was taken seriously in France, England, Germany, and Holland long before Americans saw its merit. American jazz artists toured the major cities of Europe just as American opera singers did; in Europe, they were idols well before most Americans even recognized their names.

SCHOLARS don't agree on the derivation of the word jazz or the original spelling, but the first jazz records were by the Dixieland Jass Band. One theory is that the word comes from the phonetic spelling of the first name of Mr. Alexander (as in Alexander's Ragtime Band), which, according to this theory, was Charles: Charles, Chas., Chazz, Jazz. A different suggestion is that jazz was itself derived from a slang word for semen. Another theory is that it comes from *jaiza*, a word from an African language meaning a distant rumble of drums, or from another African word meaning hurry. Possibly it came from an Arab word that means one who allures, or from a Hindi word (*jazba*) for ardent desire. They all fit; none really sounds right.

SCHOLARS even disagree about how to define the music itself. Louis Armstrong defined jazz as "My idea of how a tune should go." Any number of musicians are supposed to have said about jazz rhythm, "If you have to ask, you haven't got it." Duke Ellington put it to music: "It Don't Mean a Thing If It Ain't Got That Swing." Without a proper definition or etymology, jazz has birthed its own language that, like the music, has become part of the American mother tongue: cool, hip, hep, cat, chick, gone, solid, riff, blue, jitterbug, swing, far-out, jive, boogie, funky, beat, and a host of others.

ALL of this is food for thought, but music is food for the soul. If we can't agree about the roots of jazz, there is one thing we can agree upon: the sound, the wonderful, free, compelling, haunting, liberating sound. The sound is the melody and harmony, improvised or arranged, embroidering the beat—the steady rhythm which is the living pulse at the heart of jazz.

That pulse is an echo of our

own hearts. One of the reasons jazz is compelling is that it speaks so directly, so strongly, to our bodies as well as our souls. It is a language filled with joy yet overwhelmingly sad. Our senses overflow with the music; our feet won't stay still. We clap our hands, and our shoulders bounce up and down. Then we hear the blue notes, and we are quiet and comforted. Jazz contains the innocence of children and the sensuality of men and women. Jazz is flirtation and consummation, approach and the morning after.

THE final paradox: each jazz melody is a story whether or not it has lyrics. Jazz is an art form because each separate story rises in music from the small heart of one man or woman to touch the heart of another then another, and another, and the small and separate become universal, touching us all. No matter what jazz means, where it begins and ends, and how and why, jazz is a music we all speak.

We hope in this book that we have gone beyond the biographical details of the artists' lives to tell the story of jazz in words and music—from its beginnings at the turn of the century when Louis Armstrong was born in New Orleans, to its movement up the Mississippi to Kansas City and Chicago and east to New York, sweeping the country during the modern age of records, radio, with Benny Goodman, and the other big bands. These are stories for the jazz aficionado and the jazz newcomer. From Fats Waller playing the organ in his father's church to Dave Brubeck dreaming of meeting Benny Goodman while driving cattle on his father's ranch, these stories are legends, not because they're not true, but because, like the music, they have gone beyond individual truth to a universal art that joins us all.

LOUIS ARMSTRONG

Louis Armstrong in action.

L OUIS Armstrong was at the center of jazz, and he was a great popular entertainer. He performed with symphony orchestras and made hits of Broadway show tunes, playing on the back streets of New Orleans and in the palaces of Europe. An illiterate boy who became a giant in twentieth-century music, he was singular, inimitable, unforgettable.

M ILLIONS of people think of Armstrong as the funny, gravelly voice on records like "Hello, Dolly" and "Mack the Knife"; those records are just two of his dozens of hits on the pop charts. But Armstrong was a towering figure not only in American popular music, but also in jazz. There are those who say he was the most important figure in all of modern music.

ARMSTRONG was born at the turn of the century and grew up when ragtime was blending into jazz. One of the first jazz stars and one of the most original and successful, as well, he helped to create jazz, modeling it and remodeling it, having had a critical effect on all the music that came after it: swing and rock, easy listening and theater, radio and movies, even the classical music of such composers as Copland, Poulenc, and Milhaud. He was the sentimental buffoon of popular music—mugging on stage and off, relentlessly cheerful and ready to please, willing to sing and play almost anything, ready to laugh at himself to make us laugh, too—a lovable court jester. Jazz purists looked down their noses at Armstrong (after they'd collected his early records). It was only after his death in 1971 that he began to be recognized for what he was: one of the true musical geniuses of this century.

Louis Armstrong was born on July 4, 1900, according to the myth he loved. In fact, he was probably born a little earlier. His mother was poor and single, and it was a time when nobody kept records of the births of poor black babies. He grew up in Storyville, the poorest part of New Orleans, an area of run-down wooden shanties. He had a younger sister, but his father wasn't part of the family, and there were times when his mother wasn't there either. Sometimes Louis supported them all by singing on street corners for pennies, running errands for prostitutes and pimps, and delivering newspapers. He was buying his own clothes by the time he was ten.

ARMSTRONG'S street nickname was Gatemouth, or sometimes Dippermouth, for his wide grin. Satchmo, probably from Satchelmouth, came later, and Pops later still. His mother called him Louis, and when he grew up, that's what he preferred to be called, but millions of people called him Louie, as if he were a personal friend.

Armstrong was singing on a street corner with three other boys on New Year's Eve in 1912 or 1913 when, as part of the celebration, or to show off, or to respond to a tease or a challenge, he fired a .38 into the air. It was his mother's boyfriend's gun, and whatever his reason for firing it, he was arrested and sent to the Colored Waifs' Home to serve an indeterminate sentence.

THE home wasn't as bad as it sounds, and one of the best things about it was its brass band—a bass drum and about fifteen other instruments. The boys in the band wore long white pants, blue gabardine coats, black stockings, sneakers, and caps. They were given peppermint candy and gingerbread as a reward for playing.

The bugle was Armstrong's first instrument. He learned it at the Waif's Home in New Orleans.

They were a marching band, raising money for the Home as they paraded through the streets of New Orleans.

THEY were led by a musician named Peter Davis, and they were good. Armstrong said later that he hung around rehearsals, sitting in a corner of the band room day after day, wanting to join, wanting to learn. It took six months, but finally Davis invited him to join the band—playing tambourine. Beginners always started on percussion, because Davis believed they had to understand the rhythm before they could understand anything else. Armstrong moved to drum, then alto horn—a band version of the French horn, also known as a mellophone. When the boy who was the Home's bugler (the one who sounded the signals for meals and reveille and taps) was released, Armstrong became bugler. Finally, he was allowed to learn the cornet.

ARMSTRONG didn't learn jazz, or the blues, or even ragtime at the Home, but rather a brass-band repertory—marching songs, patriotic airs, religious songs, and old popular favorites—with brass-band techniques: pure tone, powerful sound, clean execution, showy style, and sentimental interpretation. His first training was melodic. For the rest of his life, the idea of a technically strong, rich expression of melody was at the heart of his music, above any rhythmic ideas, though he was a master of rhythm, too.

AFTER Armstrong was released from the Home, he worked days delivering coal, and nights playing music. He started in the honky-tonks, cheap bars with space for dancing and upstairs rooms for the prostitutes and their customers. He was a local kid, a familiar face—always cheerful, always ingratiating—and very often the cornetists he'd beg for a chance to play were glad to take a break for a drink or something to eat. One of the local musicians said later, "Everyone went wild over this boy in knee trousers who could play so great."

Armstrong was successful enough to buy his first cornet with ten dollars that he had borrowed from the owner of his newspaper route. He bought a beat-up instrument at a pawn shop and began working regularly. He was about seventeen years old.

Armstrong played the blues with the honky-tonk bands but soon learned about jazz. He listened to King Oliver, then the best cornetist in New Orleans. Oliver was Armstrong's idol and became his mentor and teacher. When King Oliver went to Chicago, Armstrong replaced him in Kid Ory's band. And in 1922, King Oliver brought Armstrong to Chicago.

LOUIS had already worked the riverboats on the Mississippi, making round trips from New Orleans. Now more and more blacks were making a one-way trip to Chicago. In the north, there was hope for better jobs, no Jim Crow segregation laws, and no lynchings. The audience for jazz moved north—an audience that was now white as well as black. The first jazz records in 1917 (by "The Original Dixieland Jass Band," a white group calling it jass instead of jazz) on Victor

Records were snapped up by young people across the country. Those 78s were the advance ripples of the new wave sweeping up the Mississippi.

IT was a wave that Louis Armstrong rode. He played with King Oliver at Chicago's Lincoln Gardens, the hot spot for the new music, making his first records with King Oliver's Creole Jazz Band in 1923. Those records were the first "real" jazz band discs, and their influence was enormous; for the next two decades, musicians went to school by listening to those records, in the same way that Bix Beiderbecke and Benny Goodman had learned by hearing the music firsthand at the Lincoln Gardens.

BY 1924, Armstrong had married Lil Hardin, pianist with the King Oliver band. She took charge of him—made him lose weight, buy better clothes, and, finally, quit the band, where he would always be second cornet, to find the kind of work he deserved. At the invitation of Fletcher Henderson, Armstrong moved to New York City to play with Henderson's band, which was starring at Roseland. New York was the center of the entertainment industry, a place where stars were made, where jazz was new and exploding. And Henderson's band was the best, with Coleman Hawkins on tenor sax, Buster Bailey on clarinet, and Charlie Green on trombone. With them, and with a new, more brilliant-sounding instrument—the trumpet that Henderson had suggested he try—Armstrong rose to the top.

ARMSTRONG'S early jazz records include some of the finest trumpet solos in the history of jazz. Even so, Armstrong never thought of himself as a jazz musician or a keeper of the jazz flame. He was a musician; he played beautiful music, and he made people happy—and that was what he wanted to do, making literally hundreds of recordings (78s, 45s, LPs) and more than seventy-five made it to the top of the pop charts. He worked with other people's orchestras and bands; he headed his own groups, large and small. The musicians he played with were among the best in the industry. His voice is instantly recognizable, unmistakably Armstrong. Nearly a quarter of a century after his death in 1971, his records still sell.

They are anthems of joy and musicianship.

Armstrong in a pose meant to amuse.

PROBABLY more than any other musician, Billie Holiday is the embodiment of a jazz legend. At first her unique style and great beauty were riveting. She was like a flower—like the white gardenia she wore in her hair when she performed—full of the perfume of sex, touched with a secret mystery, fragile and glowing. And like a flower, her bloom was followed by decay and darkness as she descended into drug abuse, scandal, and battles with the law. When she died in a New York City hospital, she was under arrest for possession of narcotics and was desperate for both money and friends.

HOLIDAY had fallen from grace, but in truth, she hadn't had far to fall. Her life had begun only a short metaphorical distance from where it ended: in poverty, loneliness, and great need.

Billie Holiday was born in Baltimore in 1915. Her real name was Eleanora; she was the daughter of Sadie Fagan and guitarist Clarence Holiday, who had played with Fletcher Henderson's big band, among others. Some say he was a great guitarist. He wasn't much of a father.

HOLIDAY earned her first nickel when she was six years old, scrubbing the front steps of Baltimore row houses. The happiest part of her childhood was spent doing cleaning work in a neighborhood whorehouse—the madame let her listen to Louis Armstrong and Bessie Smith records on the Victrola. When she was ten, she was sent to a home for "wayward girls" after a neighbor attempted to rape her. At fifteen she and her mother moved north, to Harlem. Holiday was put in a boardinghouse that doubled as a brothel, and she worked there as a prostitute.

In 1932, Holiday was reunited with her mother and soon after that landed a job at a local nightspot. She said later that she just asked for a job, and when the owner asked her what she could do, she said she was a dancer. After she had demonstrated that she couldn't dance, he gave her another chance, and this time she told the truth: "I'm a singer." He let her try out again, and this time

she got the job. She was paid eighteen dollars a week plus tips; she sang from midnight to 3:00 A.M. every night. When she was hired, she hadn't eaten in twenty-four hours. The first thing she did with her tips on the first night was buy a sandwich. She ate it. Then she bought a chicken and took it home.

Shortly after, two things happened that were to be repeated many times in Holiday's life: word got around about how good she was, but she had trouble keeping a job. She didn't sing the way everybody else did. Her phrasing was different; she used her voice like an instrument, the way that she had heard Louis Armstrong using his voice. Her timing was different; she sang just a little behind the beat. Using lyrics differently, she brought feeling to even the most inane words, and because she improvised, she made them her own. Singing like her idols, Bessie Smith and Louis Armstrong, she said she wanted their kind of feeling in

Lady Day.

her songs. "I don't think I'm singing. I feel like I'm playing a horn," she said about her voice. "I try to improvise like Les Young, like Louis Amrstrong, or someone else I admire. I have to change a tune to my own way of doing it. That's all I know."

THAT made the owners of the small clubs where Holiday started to sing nervous, and she went from one place to another until enough of the right people had heard her. In 1937, she was offered a spot with the new Count Basie orchestra; about a year after that, she left to sing with Artie Shaw's band. Her first records were made with pianist Teddy Wilson in 1935—their collaborations over the next three or four years include some of jazz's greatest recordings. Now, with the records and the bands, word was getting around again. She was becoming a star.

Holiday's collaboration—on records and in love—with the great tenor saxophonist Lester Young began in these years. It was Young who first called Holiday "Lady Day." She called him "the

15

president" or Prez. Holiday came home on the records they made together—she sang the way he played—and there is a kind of joy, a feeling of freedom and exuberance. About Lester Young and Teddy Wilson, Holiday said later, simply, "They played music the way I like it."

MANY of her records during that time—the late thirties—made it to the pop charts. "Carelessly," recorded in 1937, spent three weeks as the country's number-one hit and twelve weeks altogether on the charts.

In 1939, Holiday was offered a steady job at Greenwich Village's sophisticated Café Society Downtown—the "in" spot for trendy New Yorkers and the first interracial club downtown, where many jazz and popular stars got their first break. Holiday ended every set at Café Society with "Strange Fruit," a powerful and poetic comment on race relations in America—specifically the murder of southern black men by white lynching parties. "Southern trees bear a strange fruit / Blood on the leaves and blood at the root

/ Black bodies swaying in the southern breeze / Strange fruit hanging from the poplar trees." These are strong and biting words, and Holiday sang them with understated bitterness and contempt to great effect.

LIKE "Strange Fruit," "God Bless the Child" is a nonjazz song sung by a great jazz singer. A powerful indictment of the difference between the haves and the have-nots, "God Bless the Child" was another Billie Holiday anthem. ". . . The strong gets more / While the weak ones fade / Empty pockets don't ever make the grade / Mama may have / Papa may have / But God bless the child / That's got his own / That's got his own." In her autobiography Holiday wrote, "You've got to have something to eat and a little love in your life before you can hold still for anybody's damn sermon." Most of Billie Holiday's songs have to do with the way women are mistreated by men. "Strange Fruit" and "God Bless the Child" look

coldly at inhumanities we all share.

After Café Society, Holiday starred as a featured solo singer at top clubs around the country. She was beautiful and successful, but by the early forties, the decline had begun. Holiday was using heroin, injecting it every day. Pushers were part of her entourage. She wasn't reliable. There were beginning to be clubs where the owners wouldn't hire her. Her voice had begun to go.

IN 1946, Holiday detoxed for the first time. In 1947, she was arrested on a drug charge and sent to prison. After she got out, she couldn't get a cabaret card—necessary then to work in New

York clubs. Working out of town, she did some illegal dates in New York, had brief success at a Carnegie Hall concert, and was busted again in 1956, at this point addicted to alcohol as well as heroin.

Holiday's last appearance was in May of 1959. Hospitalized again, while there, she was arrested for possession of narcotics. She died on July 17, 1959.

BILLIE Holiday said she wanted to sound like Bessie Smith and Louis Armstrong. But listening to her, only one person comes to mind: Billie Holiday. Her voice was unique, and so was her singing. She was a musician's musician. Her range certainly wasn't great—"It just go up a bit and come down a little bit," she said about her voice—but her sound was intimate and intense, raw and vulnerable. Her voice is full of pain and full of joy, full of darkness and full of heart. To listen to Billie Holiday is to see the dark side of the moon.

DUKE ELLINGTON

WHEN the New York Times featured Duke Ellington's obituary on page one of its May 25, 1974, edition, the headline phrase was simple: "Master of Music." Although the wording was accurate, coined specifically for the occasion and deserved beyond comparison to any twentieth-century musical figure, classical or jazz, the description amounted to less than the sum of the master's achievements. For the man whose career lasted from 1918 into the 1970s, who composed a staggering number of works, and whose arrangements led the way for virtually every musician who came after him, the word "unique" should somehow have gotten into the copy.

Edward Kennedy Ellington, nicknamed Duke from early childhood, was born April 29, 1899, in Washington, D.C. He took piano lessons as a child and during high school began playing at True Reformers Hall, later sitting in for pianist Lester Dishman at Washington's Poodle Dog Café. While there he wrote his first instrumental, "Soda Fountain Rag," followed by his first song with lyrics, "What Are You Going to Do When the Bed Breaks Down?"

PROFICIENT in art as well as music, Ellington won a contest for poster design sponsored by the NAACP, and was offered a scholarship to Pratt Institute in New York. Instead he left high school, continued with the piano (while studying harmony independently), and started his own sign-painting business.

THE road to becoming leader of his own band was highlighted by performances for a number of musical organizations in the Washington area: Daniel Doyle, Doc Perry, Elmer Snowden—he even appeared as one of five pianists in Russell Wooding's thirty-four-piece orchestra. When Duke Ellington started his own small group in 1918, alto saxophonist Otto Hardwick and trumpeter Arthur Whetsol joined him, as did later star drummer Sonny Greer the following year. His group became one of many bands in the national ferment that produced early music by the Original Dixieland Jass Band, King Oliver, and Louis Armstrong. New Orleans, Chicago, and New York were the main centers for jazz, so it was to the Big Apple that Ellington's Serenaders traveled in 1922. Along with Snowden's group, the Washing-tonians, Ellington and his sidemen took up residency at the Hollywood Club in New York.

Duke Ellington in a Bluebird publicity photograph. What could be smoother?

RECORDINGS assisted Ellington in his rise to leadership of the Washingtonians: in November 1924, with clarinetist Bubber Miley and trombonist Charlie Irvis, the band recorded its first two sides, "Choo Choo" and "Rainy Nights." The following

New York City's Duke Ellington Traffic Circle, dedicated in 1995. There's also a Duke Ellington Boulevard. Chester Higgins, Jr., *New York Times* Pictures.

year Ellington and Joe Trent wrote the score for a New York revue, *Chocolate Kiddies*. Ellington then began a series of tours through New England that included extended appearances at the Charleshurst Ballroom in Salem, Massachusetts. Back in New York,

the group played at the Flamingo, Harry Richman's, Ciro's, and the Hollywood Club—now renamed the Kentucky—along with numerous appearances at theaters. A strongly identifiable Ellington sound developed during the years from 1925 to 1927. Bluesy parallel harmonies; tonal clusters, sometimes dissonant (often unworldly), utilizing the individual colors of his selected musicians; and precision overall—these became his trademarks. Names such as Don Redman, Prince Robinson, and Harry Carney graced the band during these times of expanded performances. Adelaide Hall handled the vocal on "Creole Love Call," while the band recorded such standards to be as "East St. Louis Toodle-Oo" and "Black and Tan Fantasy" dur-

ing their first Victor dates (New York and Camden, New Jersey) in October 1927.

THE crowning move came on December 4, 1927, when Duke Ellington and his Kentucky Club Orchestra set up residency at Harlem's famous Cotton Club. It was here that the band became nationally known through records, major theater performances (the Palace, the Paramount, the Savoy Ballroom), and, in 1929, their first Broadway musical, *Show Girl*, with music by George Gershwin. During August 1930, they traveled to California for engagements and the filming of a spot in the highly publicized movie, *Check and Double Check*.

DUKE Ellington's orchestra left the Cotton Club in February 1931. During that year they toured extensively, with long stopovers in Boston and California, before returning to the Paramount in New York. Dozens of Ellington sides were recorded in the city and at RCA Victor's Camden studios: "Rockin' in Rhythm," "Creole Rhapsody," "Echoes of the Jungle,"

"Limehouse Blues"—the list is impressive.

ON June 9, 1933, the orchestra arrived in England for performances at the London Palladium (also in Liverpool and Glasgow) before playing a series of concerts in Paris. It was fertile ground for American jazz as collectors and fans gave Duke Ellington and his famous orchestra standing ovations everywhere. By this time some of his most celebrated sidemen had joined the band: Johnny Hodges on alto sax, Cootie Williams on trumpet, Lawrence Brown and Juan Tizol on trombones.

Duke Ellington in a mellow mood, RCA Victor, 1957.

IT was an all-star assemblage, including vocalist Ivie Anderson, that Duke took on his first southern United States tour later in 1933. That was also the year of his first Chicago Victor sessions, ending on January 9 and 10, 1934: "Dear Old Southland," "Dallas Doings," "Delta Serenade" (Texas and Louisiana had been visited on the tour), plus the first recording of his all-time hit, "Solitude." Ellington's next round of Hollywood sessions coincided with the films *Symphony in Black*, *Murder at the Vanities*, and *Belle of the Nineties*—with Mae West as vocalist!

AFTER a Canadian tour and several New York sessions with the Brunswick label in 1935, Ellington returned to Chicago for a residency at the Congress Hotel, then resumed at the Cotton Club on March 20, 1937. The following year he wrote the music for the ballet *City Woman* while recuperating from hernia surgery. His ever-growing musical pallette was displayed on new tours of France, Belgium, and Scandinavia, where his following numbered in the

hundreds of thousands. His best-known compositions from this period are "Caravan," "Echoes of Harlem," "Sophisticated Lady," and an extended work, "Reminiscing in Tempo," dedicated to the memory of his mother.

In 1940, pianist Billy Strayhorn joined the band as staff arranger; with a style similar to Ellington's, he was soon cowriting many of their works, including the band's theme song, "Take the A Train." The addition of trumpeter Rex Stewart, tenor saxophonist Ben Webster, and bassist Jimmy Blanton brought the 1940–42 band to what was arguably the height of jazz performances anywhere. New repertoire included "Perdido," "Chelsea Bridge," "Jump for Joy" (the title song for the 1941 civil rights show in Los Angeles), "Jack the Bear," "Bojangles," "Portrait of Bert Williams", and Duke Ellington's masterpiece to date: "Black, Brown, and Beige," a musical history of American blacks (including work songs and the music of contemporary Harlem), presented at Carnegie Hall in 1943. Al

Hibbler became Ellington's main vocalist from 1943 to 1951, replacing Herb "Flamingo" Jeffries and the versatile Ivie Anderson. Touring continued unabated, with full-house residencies in Chicago, Hollywood, and the Zanzibar in New York. Carnegie Hall concerts became a nearly annual event, with such major works as "Deep South Suite" (1946) and the Strayhorn-influenced "Liberian Suite" (1947). After a brief hospital stay, Ellington toured British music halls with vocalist Kay Davis and trumpeter-vocalist Ray Nance during the summer of 1948. But times were changing for jazz.

THE decline of big bands after World War II, crippling record bans in 1942 and 1948, the rise of bebop and its improvisational small-group orientation—these and related economic factors gradually, but effectively, ended a musical era. For Duke Ellington it meant greater emphasis on his many other skills—

This poster was a fund raiser for Daytop. Pete Seeger is in the middle, and in the circles around him are the Grateful Dead, Janis Ian, Hugh Masekela, and (overcircle bottom left) Duke Ellington. Courtesy of Ned Moran, Hudson Valley Rock and Roll Museum of Art.

including film scores for *The Asphalt Jungle* in 1950 and the award-winning *Anatomy of a Murder* in 1959. Tenor saxophonist Paul Gonsalves was added to Ellington's band in 1950, followed by trumpeters Clark Terry and William Alonzo "Cat" Anderson,

giving the ensemble a more modern orientation and a greater focus on instrumentals. After a somewhat commercial phase with Capitol Records in 1953–54, Ellington signed with Columbia to record live at the Newport Jazz Festival on July 6 and 7, 1956. This resulted in a brilliant album that featured Gonsalves in a tumultuous last-set performance of "Diminuendo and Crescendo in Blue": twenty-seven solo tenor choruses that absolutely rival Ravel's *Bolero*—driving ever harder toward the final crescendo—followed by seven climactic orchestral choruses led by Anderson's soaring trumpet. The effect on the audience was gal-vanic, and the recording captures it all, perhaps the supreme moment in the history of the festival!

In the autumn of 1958, Ellington's band made a triumphant return to London, the first of several British tours that lasted into the sixties. Film scores, such as *Paris Blues* in 1961 and *Assault on a Queen* in 1966, kept the large-scale muses busy, while orchestra tours to the Far East, the Middle East, India, and South America were prominent features throughout the decade. In 1970, Duke composed "The River" for the American Ballet, then led a particularly far-ranging tour to Japan, Australia, and New Zealand. In 1973, he completed his autobiography, *Music Is My Mistress*, and on May 24, 1974, Duke Ellington died of cancer and pneumonia at the Columbia Presbyterian Medical Center in New York City.

TODAY regarded as America's greatest composer in any genre, Ellington led his orchestra for more than fifty years. He was, and probably will always remain, incomparable in our national annals.

The sophisticated gentleman: Duke Ellington.

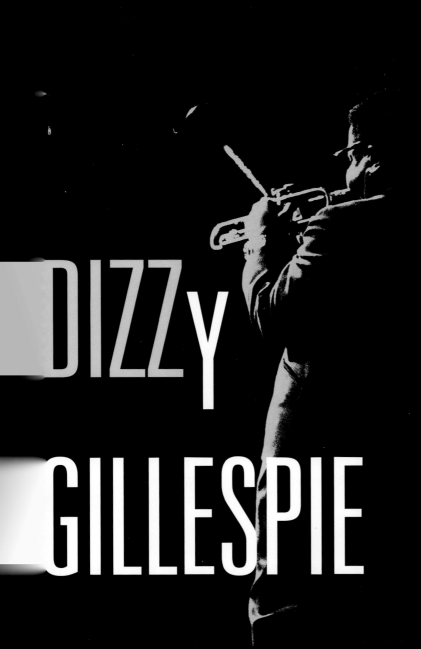

DIZZY GILLESPIE

RARELY in any field has a personality combined such vision and achievement as John Birks "Dizzy" Gillespie. Born October 21, 1917, in Cheraw, South Carolina, Gillespie began studying music early (his father played several instruments) and formed a teenage trio with a pianist and a drummer. He won a scholarship to Laurinburg Institute in North Carolina but left before his senior year, moving to Philadelphia in 1935, where he played with Frank Fairfax's band.

GILLESPIE'S first break came in 1937, when he joined Teddy Hill and his NBC Orchestra in New York. This prestigious group included Russell Procope, Duke Ellington's alto sax star for nearly thirty years starting in 1945, and Dicky Wells, later Count Basie's lead trombonist. In no time the nineteen-year-old Gillespie found himself on a celebrated tour of Europe, then recording in New York for RCA Bluebird Records, with the band.

HILL'S venue was the Savoy Ballroom in Harlem, a virtual revolving stage of star attractions for the jazz world. In the summer of 1939, Gillespie joined Cab Calloway and his orchestra, another stellar group that included tenor saxophonist Chu Berry, bassist Milt Hinton, and drummer Cozy Cole. In relation to mainstream trumpeters of the day, Gillespie's tone was criticized as anemic, a factor which may have contributed indirectly to his development as a virtuoso improviser, arranger, and composer.

IT was during the Calloway period that Dizzy Gillespie began experimenting with the harmonic and scale elements that would set him apart from the main-

Dizzy Gillespie and his famous angled horn.

stream—and starting in 1941, on his own, arranging music for such ensembles as those of Charlie Barnet, Ella Fitzgerald, Fletcher Henderson, and Woody Herman.

In 1942, he briefly led his own small band at the Down Beat Club in Philadelphia before joining Earl Hines's orchestra, where he teamed with a like-minded alto sax player named Charlie Parker.

Iconoclasm was in the air, but before it blossomed into full-scale revolution, much performing and real work were to come. For Gillespie and Parker, after-hours sessions at Minton's Playhouse in Harlem provided the lab where whole-tone scales, altered (ninth, eleventh, even thirteenth) chords, and an entirely novel technique of performing (with bursts and cascades of sixteenth notes) were born. Their driving styles and imaginations brought all of this together—into the free and fantastic realm known as bebop.

BILLY Eckstine's big band, where Gillespie landed in 1944, was a highly active seedbed for new musical ideas: even ballads took on an eerie beauty under the harmonic influence of bop. When Gillespie and Parker made their own historic first recordings the following year, a new age of jazz was born—one of unprecedented virtuosity, musical depth, and complexity. When blown to big-band proportions, the effect upon listeners was awesome.

Dizzy Gillespie led his big band for most of the next five years. "Things to Come," recorded for Musicraft in July 1946, was the apogee of the new style: five trumpets, three trombones, five saxes, and full rhythm (including John Lewis, piano; Milt Jackson, vibes; Ray Brown, bass; and Kenny Clarke, drums) comprise the dense atonal scoring. The tempo is incredibly fast (even Dizzy has trouble keeping up during his rangy solos), and the effect is hair raising. With "Manteca," recorded for Victor in December 1947, he established Afro-Cuban jazz with a smaller, more intimate rhythmic ensemble. It was a time of firsts!

Gillespie's career after 1950 was devoted mainly to small groups. He toured Europe and the United States with Norman Granz's Jazz at the Philharmonic and recorded copiously—for a while with his own label, DeeGee

Records. He returned to the big-band format with two wide-ranging international tours for the U.S. State Department in 1956, later retracing this acclaimed route with his own quintet. In 1971–72, he was featured in an all-star touring group called the Giants of Jazz, a gig that lasted into the 1980s.

From its inception bebop had a humorous, somewhat ironic side—jazz as entertainment as well as an avant-garde art form. Dizzy Gillespie brought the two strains together conclusively through his invention of a trumpet with its bell extended upward at a forty-five-degree angle. Since he added to his signature perfor-

mances hugely inflated cheeks and a frequent beret, his onstage persona delighted and captured the attention of millions whose familiarity with real jazz might otherwise have been limited.

In 1978, Gillespie appeared at Jimmy Carter's White House Jazz Party. In a gesture toward the president's farming back-ground, he induced Carter to sing a chorus of "Salt Peanuts," Dizzy's only chart single, recorded with Charlie Parker for the Guild label during that bygone glory year of 1945. It was a crowning moment for the musician from Cheraw, who had done simply everything in his chosen field with brilliance, humor, insight, and imagination, and who single-handedly had redefined the limits of musical style. Dizzy Gillespie died in Englewood, New Jersey, on January 6, 1993.

CHARLIE PARKER

I F melody is the face of jazz and the beat is its backbone, then improvisation is surely its heart and soul. Since pianist/violinist James Reese Europe recorded his earliest riffs in the 1910s, improvisation has grown and expanded into unimagined realms. Louis Armstrong and Lester Young brought it into the modern era; when Charlie Parker and Dizzy Gillespie invented bebop in the forties, all boundaries were shattered. Charles Christopher Parker was born August 29, 1920, in Kansas City, Missouri. He was largely self-taught; after playing baritone sax in high school, he dropped out at age fourteen and started appearing professionally on alto sax—a change reflecting the influence of altoist Buster Smith. His earliest name-band experience was with Harlan Leonard's Rockets in Kansas City, where Smith and arranger Tadd Dameron soon extended the limits of mainstream jazz. Parker's big break came with Jay McShann's famed orchestra in 1938.

Although McShann's style was mainstream, several solos recorded by Parker during their 1941–42 sessions for Decca showed the changes that were to come. His stylistic variations were influenced by tenor saxophonist Lester Young, whose distinctive improvisations with Count Basie's orchestra dated from that group's own 1936–37 beginnings in Kansas City.

I T was a time and place of ferment: when visiting New York with McShann, Parker met innovative drummer Kenny Clarke and pioneer pianist Thelonious Monk, who decisively influenced his playing. After a brief backward step with Noble Sissle's entertainment-oriented band, Charlie Parker stepped into the future by signing on with Earl Hines's orchestra—playing tenor sax for a while—then with Billy Eckstine's band, both nurseries of the nascent bop style.

P ARKER'S musical soul mate in the Eckstine ensemble was Dizzy Gillespie. At Minton's Playhouse, a club organized by bandleader Teddy Hill, where they met with Clarke, Monk, and others, modern jazz was born. Lightninglike melodic runs, harmonic shifts, dissonance, playing at the very limit of their instruments' capabilities, and all executed with astonishing technique—these were the hallmarks of bebop. It was also a way of reclaiming jazz for black artists, creating a style with which white musicians, by then having won most of the mainstream jobs, would not be able to compete. It worked, at least for a while.

After the 1942 recording ban (brought on by the American Federation of Musicians union) was lifted in the mid-1940s, Parker and Gillespie toured together spreading the new wave through 78-rpm discs, mostly combo performances, but later through dazzling big-band releases as well. By this time Parker had acquired the nicknames "Bird" and "Yardbird": like the shorthand of the music itself, bop was the province of Diz and Bird, and a select few others who could keep up with them.

For Charlie Parker, sadly, keeping up involved increasing addiction to heroin, and a breakdown in mid-1946 led to several months in a California hospital. When released, he took part in Jazz at the Philharmonic concerts with Lester Young and Coleman Hawkins—the three greatest saxophonists of the century on one stage. Parker played Paris in 1949 and toured Scandinavia in 1950. In the latter year, he broke new ground again, recording with strings and woodwinds, Latin bands, and choral groups. His most memorable performances of

1950, however, occurred with his own quintet at St. Nicholas Arena, and with Gillespie, Monk, bassist Curly Russell, and drummer Buddy Rich under Jazz at the Philharmonic founder Norman Granz's direction. The high point

Left: Charlie Parker with Dizzy Gillespie (left) and Billy Eckstine (right) *courtesy of the Frank Driggs Collection.*

Above: Charlie Parker and his saxophone.

of Parker's later career came with the 1953 album, *Quintet of the Year*, with Gillespie, pianist Bud Powell, bassist Charlie Mingus, and drummer Max Roach. It featured several bebop standards such as "Night in Tunisia" and "Salt Peanuts," and showed much of the solid improvisational work that had made him famous throughout the world.

SINCE the advent of compact discs, numerous performances have come to light from private tapes of this period. But many show how ravaged his superb talent had become, and it wasn't long before it was stilled altogether. Charlie Parker died in New York on March 12, 1955. He once said, "There's always so much more to be done in music. It's so vast. And that's why I'm always trying to develop, to find new and better ways of saying things musically." As Parker's fans continue to listen into the 1990s, they can all agree with a phrase that began in 1955: "Bird lives."

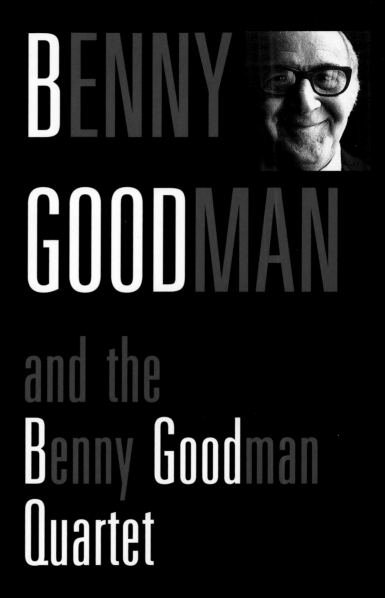

BENNY GOODMAN
and the
Benny Goodman
Quartet

THERE was a kind of royalty in the big swing bands that evolved out of jazz: Count Basie, Duke Ellington. The King of Swing was Benny Goodman.

Royalty is a long way from Goodman's beginnings. He was born in 1909 in Chicago, the ninth of twelve children. His parents were turn-of-the-century immigrants from Eastern Europe and poor—"I can remember when we lived in a basement without heat during the winter, and a couple of times when there wasn't anything to eat. I don't mean much to eat. I mean anything," he later recalled.

GOODMAN'S father loved music; he took his children to free band concerts in the park, the first music Benny remembered hearing. His father came to think the kids might be able to bring in a little extra money if they could play; he found a professional musician who taught at a local temple without charge, and the synagogue loaned them instruments. The biggest of the Goodman boys was given a tuba or a trombone; the next one, a trumpet or an alto horn. Benny was the smallest, and they handed him a clarinet.

THE swing movement was a kind of craze that grew out of jazz. Fletcher Henderson, Duke Ellington, Jean Goldkette, Paul Whiteman—they all had big jazz bands with brass and reed sections and jazz soloists. But it was Benny Goodman's band that transformed swing into a national phenomenon. He'd been working in other people's bands, playing small dates, making records, when, in 1934, he formed his own group, and they auditioned for a spot on a new Saturday-night radio show to be called "Let's Dance."

Radio had come into its own during these early days of the depression. Once the radio was paid for, listening was free entertainment, and that mattered a lot. A CBS survey in 1934 showed that over 90 percent of American homes had at least one radio; the average listening time was four-and-a-half hours a day. An NBC survey revealed that dance music was the most popular kind of program on the air.

"Let's Dance" originated in

Quartet member Teddy Wilson at the piano.

NBC's Studio 8H—Toscanini's famous broadcast home and the place from which today's *Saturday Night Live* is broadcast. The program used three different orchestras in order to appeal to the widest possible audience. One was Kel Murray's sweet band, for commercial dance music. The second was a Latin band—Xavier Cugat's—for rumbas. The third was a hot dance band for teenagers.

THE hottest bands of the day— those led by Duke Ellington, Fletcher Henderson, Jimmie Lunceford, and Chick Webb— were all black. They were great, but the network wouldn't use them. The Dorsey brothers were white but not available. Benny Goodman got the job. He hired Fletcher Henderson to do his arrangements. Henderson's work had the free feeling of jazz: whole sections of the orchestra sounded like single soloists; there was an exciting beat and a feeling of drive.

LET'S Dance" was broadcast live from coast to coast for three hours, beginning at 10:30 P.M. in New York. Goodman's band went on the air last, when radio executives thought middle-aged listeners would have gone to bed, but the young audience most eager for the new, hot sound would still be listening.

When the show folded because a strike caused the sponsor not to renew, a tour was organized that would take the Goodman band across the country. Their appearances weren't successful—audiences didn't like the swing sound. By the time they reached California, Goodman was near despair; Denver, he said, "was the most humiliating experience of my life." The band members were all completely demoralized.

BUT at the Palomar Ballroom in Los Angeles, there were lines reaching around the block, waiting to get in. Goodman began the evening cautiously, emphasizing sweet commercial tunes during the first set. There was no response; the band was dying again. Someone—Bunny Berigan or Gene Krupa—said to Goodman, "We might as well go down swinging." So the next set opened with the Fletcher Henderson arrangements. "That first big roar from the crowd was one of the sweetest sounds I ever heard in my life," Goodman said.

ONE of the theories proposed later was that the kids on the West Coast, because of the time difference in the radio broadcasts, were the only ones who were still awake when the Goodman band came on. They had learned to love its music.

The Palomar Ballroom show took place on August 21, 1935, and that date is often referred to as the birthday of swing. In fact, of course, swing had been around for years. Three years earlier Duke Ellington had said loud and clear for the whole world to hear, if they were listening: "It don't mean a thing if it ain't got that swing."

In the early thirties, the depression, coupled with the end of Prohibition, had changed the mood of the country— nightclubs and

The RCA album *This is Benny Goodman.*

30

bathtub gin and hot jazz had begun to seem frivolous, unaffordable, wrong. Sweet, sentimental songs filled the gap for a lot of people, but there's always a need, especially among young people, for dynamic, rhythmic music. Swing fell into that category. Goodman was the first to make it popular on a national level.

T HE Benny Goodman Quartet was a by-product of the Benny Goodman band. Benny had been playing at the Roosevelt Grill. One night in June, after work, he drove out to Forest Hills to a party given by Red Norvo and his wife, Mildred Bailey. One of the guests was Teddy Wilson, a young black piano player. Bailey suggested they join forces for a couple of numbers with her cousin, a drummer, who kept time that night with wire brushes on an empty suitcase. "Teddy and I began to play as though we were thinking with the same brain," Goodman said later. They played until dawn;

Gene Krupa, the great jazz drummer.

their musical rapport was almost telepathic. Their later collaboration with Billie Holiday on "I Wished on the Moon," "Miss Brown to You," and "What a Little Moonlight Can Do," produced some of the most enduring records in all of jazz.

T EDDY Wilson was the son of the head of the English department at Tuskegee Institute in Alabama; his mother was chief librarian there. He was born in 1912 and became one of the most

influential instrumentalists of the swing era, taking his place on the time line of great pianists from Jelly Roll Morton to the stride players to Fats Waller to Earl Hines, Art Tatum, Oscar Peterson, and all those who came after.

E LEVEN days after the Wilson-Holiday recording date, Goodman brought Wilson and Gene Krupa into the RCA Victor recording studios to make the first Benny Goodman Trio sides. With Krupa's hot brushes urging them on, Wilson and Goodman worked together even more closely than they had before. Their interwoven phrases have an elegance and cool virtuosity that resulted in the birth of the phrase "chamber jazz."

Krupa burst onto the jazz scene as the Benny Goodman band's drummer. Probably more than anyone else, he made the drums a popular solo instrument and brought drummers into the spotlight. The band's recording of

31

credited Zutty Singleton and Baby Dodds as major influences on his drumming style.

THE trio became a quartet when Lionel Hampton was added on vibes. Hampton was the first jazz musician to make the vibraphone a primary instrument—before him it had been, for the most part, a novelty, something drummers used for an occasional bing or bong. He had picked it up almost by accident, as a seventeen-year-old drummer with a group backing Louis Armstrong. There was a vibe in the studio where they were recording, and one day he used it for a brief ad-lib introduction. Adrian Rollini had played vibes before him, but it took Hampton's dynamism and range to give the instrument jazz validity.

HAMPTON was playing with his own small group at a bar in Los Angeles when Goodman dropped in one night to hear this musician everyone in his band was talking about. According to Hampton, Goodman sat at a table, looking amused at the idea of a solo vibraphone. But Hampton's playing was inspired that night, and after about half an hour, Goodman came over and asked if he could sit in. The place was supposed to close between two and three in the morning; they played until five. The next night Goodman came back with Wilson and Krupa and some other musicians from the band, and they all played together, again until five or six in the morning. Then Benny asked Hampton if he'd like to make a record. "Man," said Hampton later, "I was really gassed." At eleven o'clock the next morning, Goodman called Hampton and asked him to come on down to the RCA studios. He

"Sing, Sing, Sing," one of their many classics, is a prime example of an extended—and great—jazz solo in swing. Krupa, born in Chicago in 1909, was studying to be a priest when he left college to play with Chicago bands. He

ıt of bed, rushed over to
rabbed the vibes, and
the studio. The band
ling, but at the end of
n, Lionel Hampton did
—"Moonglow"—with the
as one of those natural
t was just meant to be,
of the trio all over
enny Goodman said. The
ne was born: the Benny
Quartet.
Benny Goodman first
d Teddy Wilson for the
he did something much
n add a great pianist to
great band. He broke
olor line. Adding Lionel
to create the quartet
back that much further.
hundreds—thou-
examples of the way
was segregated: the
ausicians' union had two
black, one white.
sicians played in the
clubs on New York's
et, but black patrons
velcome. White musi-
he lucrative dance-hall
dates; black musicians
ck clubs and made

"race" records, a separate category in record-company catalogs.
There was a "black" sound and a
"white" sound, matching the sep-
aration in the very bloodstream of
American society—blacks and
whites lived apart, worked apart,
played apart, went to school and
even to church apart. Black
music—as it still does—became
popular with whites, but when it
did, it was also played by them.

ENNY Goodman crossed the
invisible line, and he did so
nervously and with no great
conviction to help him as he worried. He did it because he and
Teddy Wilson played so well
together. There was no great nega-
tive reaction, but neither was the
problem over. For a long time,
blacks and whites playing together remained sufficiently rare,
so that the instances when they
did can be picked out and celebrated: Billie Holiday singing
with Artie Shaw; Lena Horne performing with Charlie Barnet; Hot
Lips Page playing trumpet with
Artie Shaw; and a few others. It
was even rarer for a black band to
include white sidemen. It wasn't

until World War II because of the
scarcity of available musicians
that the walls really began to

crumble, if not to finally fall.

LACK and white, the Benny
Goodman Quartet made beautiful music together. Before
they began jamming, small-group
jazz had virtually disappeared—
with Goodman bearing no small
part of the responsibility for that
change. The quartet did much to
bring small jazz groups back,
albeit with different instruments
and playing new music. Their
tunes took a cue from the band's
music; they played standards, cur-
rent pop hits, and some originals
written for Goodman.

The trio and the quartet

played as part of the Goodman band—separate numbers, stage center; the audience listened instead of dancing. What it heard was dazzling: a group that played with fire and authority, warmth and richness. These musicians put small-group jazz right back on the map, and you can still find it there today, more than half a century later.

GENE Krupa left Goodman to start his own big band in 1938; the next year Teddy Wilson left. In 1940, Hampton did the same. There were periodic reunions over the years; they didn't always work. The Benny Goodman legacy came from those first few years—the Carnegie Hall Concert (in 1938, the first big-band jazz concert in that great hall)—their records, radio shows, tours, even a movie.

Benny Goodman—who marked another cultural milestone in 1962 when he became the first American to take jazz to the Soviet Union since Sidney Bechet in the twenties—built bridges between jazz and classical music as well as between whites and blacks, and Americans and Russians. He recorded Alec Templeton's "Bach Goes to Town," and clarinet pieces by Bartok, Mozart, Copland, Hindemith, and Debussy, whose La Mer he recorded in 1948 as "Beyond the Sea."

GOODMAN listened to music by John Coltrane and the Grateful Dead, among others, but his style never really changed. He didn't like amplification; he thought rock and roll was an immature musical form. The word "nostalgia" was used more and more when Benny Goodman played in the fifties, sixties, seventies, even the eighties. He died on June 13, 1986, two weeks after his seventy-seventh birthday. His clarinet was in his hand. He had been playing Mozart.

THE music world is strewn with fine pianists. The most basic, popular instrument of childhood has been, unsurprisingly, the cornerstone of jazz and classical repertoire for decades. Its leading virtuosi would fill an encyclopedia, so it becomes a fine puzzle to select the best of them for *Jazz Legends*.

With Oscar Emmanuel Peterson, born August 15, 1925, in Montreal, the choice could hardly be better. This master of lightly swinging progressive jazz was classically trained. The child of West Indian parents, he studied trumpet early but took up the piano when he contracted tuberculosis. At the age of fourteen, he was performing on Canadian radio.

THE influence of Art Tatum diverted him from the classics, and Peterson was soon playing in Montreal jazz clubs. In 1949, the prodigy went to New York, where he immediately found an audience for his talents—at Carnegie Hall with Jazz at the Philharmonic.

Although he had recorded for RCA Canada, Peterson was signed to the Verve label by his manager, Norman Granz. Tours with Jazz at the Philharmonic followed. After recording for Verve in 1950, he formed a group with bassist Ray Brown and guitarist Irving Ashford. They performed in an updated Nat Cole Trio style, with Peterson trying an occasional vocal *á la Cole*. Between 1951

Oscar Peterson on the Pablo album *In Russia*.

and 1958 (with guitarist Herb Ellis after 1953), Peterson toured widely and recorded with such artists as Dizzy Gillespie, Lester Young, and vibraphonist Lionel Hampton, with whom the trio sounded like a dynamic rhythm section. From 1959–65, drummer Ed Thigpen replaced Ellis.

IN 1961, Granz sold Verve to the MGM label; as a result, Peterson began a broader exploration of pop, film and big-band repertoire. His *Night Train* and *Bursting Out* albums crowned the new affiliation, the latter arranged by saxophonist Ernie Wilkins, who had orchestrated for Count Basie, Morgana King, and others.

In 1964, Brown and Thigpen were replaced by bassist Sam Jones and drummer Louis Hayes; during the period that followed, Oscar Peterson often toured England, most successfully with Ella Fitzgerald. The years 1964–68 were spent on the Mercury label where, during debut sessions, Peterson recorded his ambitious "Canadiana Suite."

YEARS with the German MPS label featured more and more solo recordings, whose success prompted Peterson to abandon the trio format in 1972. The following year Norman Granz signed him to the new Pablo jazz label. It was to prove a gold mine of rich, diversified live performances with singer Sarah Vaughan; trumpeters Dizzy

Gillespie, Clark Terry, and Freddie Hubbard; guitarist Joe Pass; and bassist Niels-Henning Pederson. The high point was re-creating all the stages of Peterson's career in a three-album series titled *The History of an Artist*. Oscar Peterson has also become one of the most successful jazz artists on television, where his intelligent, lilting style has won millions of fans worldwide.

Ella Fitzgerald sings with Oscar Peterson. This Pablo album was produced by Norman Granz.

ELLA FITZG

ELLA Fitzgerald is known as "America's First Lady of Song," but the truth is probably a little less democratic than that. She's royalty.

Fitzgerald is unsurpassed. And she makes it sound so simple. Purity of tone, warmth of style, respect for melody, joy in singing—all that is part of what makes her so great, so accessible, so easy to love. Fitzgerald is like the other side of Billie Holiday (and they were *the* jazz singers of the thirties)—light to Holiday's darkness, laughter to despair, sunshine to moonlight.

LIFE hasn't come easily to Fitzgerald, though music has. She was born in Newport News, Virginia, in 1917 or 1918. When she was three, her mother and stepfather, a Portuguese immigrant, moved to Yonkers, New York. She grew up listening to the radio, loving especially Bing Crosby and the Boswell sisters. She told all her friends that she, too, was going to be a star someday. It didn't seem likely.

FITZGERALD was fifteen when her mother died; shortly after, an aunt took her away from her stepfather—there is a possibility of child abuse—to live in Harlem. There she became a child of the streets, a dropout and a numbers runner; she worked for a while as a lookout for a whorehouse. She was picked up by the authorities and sent to an orphanage, but she ran away and went back on the streets, where she survived by singing for pennies and sleeping wherever she could.

At seventeen Fitzgerald won an Amateur Night competition at the Apollo Theater. The prize was a week with the regular stage show. It didn't happen: she was dirty, she didn't have the right kind of clothes, and she smelled bad. Two months later she won the same competition at the rival Harlem Opera House. Here she did get the week's work—without pay, but with some new clothes.

Fitzgerald was introduced to bandleader Fletcher Henderson; he said he'd call, but he didn't. Someone else took her to bandleader Chick Webb, but he said he wasn't interested in girl singers. He hadn't heard her sing yet. According to the legend, she was smuggled into his dressing room, she sang for him, and he turned out to be interested in this girl singer.

NEXT to be convinced was Webb's manager. "Listen to the voice," Webb is supposed to have said; "don't look at her." She didn't look good—she was big and awkward, and she

wasn't dressed right. But if Chick Webb's manager closed his eyes or looked at the ceiling, he heard what we all have for well over half a century: the sound of honey. Still seventeen, Fitzgerald became the girl singer for the Chick Webb band, performing at the Savoy Ballroom, the swingingest dance spot in New York City.

In 1938, Ella Fitzgerald and

The beautiful Ella Fitzgerald. A Jack Vartoogian photograph.

Chick Webb recorded "A-Tisket, A-Tasket." Fitzgerald had cowritten the lyrics with Al Freeman; the song was a smash, and the record was number one on the pop charts for ten weeks—and remained on the charts for nineteen. It later was selected for the NARAS (National Academy of Recording Arts and Sciences, responsible for the Grammy Awards) Hall of Fame.

SILLY songs were a staple of the late thirties and early forties—tunes like "Mairzy Doats," "Hut Sut Ralston," and "Three Little Fishies" were all Hit Paraders—in jazz just as much as in popular music. Fitzgerald had the perfect voice for her silly smash: she sang "A-Tisket" like a little girl, hitching her voice up, singing the lyrics straight but giving them a sexy undertone at the same time. The result was that Fitzgerald and the Chick Webb band were now at the top.

CHICK Webb became Fitzgerald's legal guardian; he was her musical guardian as well. His back was hunched, the result of a crippling tuberculosis of the

spine, but this drummer had enough energy and spirit for two. He took care of his protégé, made sure she bought the right dresses, and helped to shape and guide her talent as she and it grew.

When Webb died in 1939, Fitzgerald became, at twenty-one, the leader of the Chick Webb band and its reason for continuing success. She was respected as a musical equal by the members of the band, and she held them together for the next three years—an unheard-of accomplishment for a woman at that time—or even since. How many women can you think of who have led popular or jazz bands? It's an accomplishment that Fitzgerald didn't aim for; it was thrust upon her by Moe

Gale, Webb's manager and then hers for a time. Fitzgerald wasn't aggressive; quite the contrary. Many who knew her in those years speak of her innocence and naivité, even childishness. She was relatively passive with her managers—Gale, and later Norman Granz and Milt Gabler, who produced her Decca recordings. Even so she was able to hold the Webb band together until World War II, when, like many another dance band, it expired.

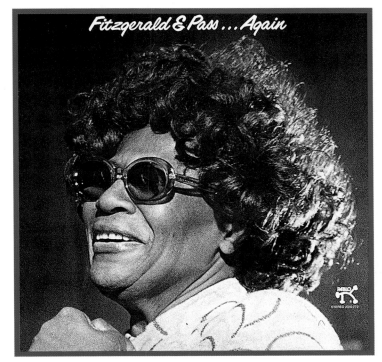

It was in the forties that bop began, and Fitzgerald grew with it, becoming a great scat singer. Her "How High the Moon" is a jazz classic. In the late forties, Norman Granz, impresario and head of Verve records, arranged a Jazz at the Philharmonic tour with Fitzgerald as star. In 1956, he won her away from Decca and began the series of Verve recordings that are still absolute and definitive classics. He recorded Fitzgerald with lush strings, with intimate trios and quartets, and with the Jazz at the Philharmonic's swinging, hard-driving horns. In the series of *Songbook*

albums, Fitzgerald recorded the Cole Porter, Rodgers and Hart, Gershwin, Ellington, and Irving Berlin repertoires. She brought her exquisite phrasing, wide range, lilting swing, and warm sound to America's favorite songs—the jazz feeling combined with great standards—and the results are still unsurpassed. Fitzgerald, who won the Down Beat poll twenty times, has

reached out with her warmth and style to millions who might otherwise have been strangers to jazz. She has given us a half century of brilliant music making.

Opposite page: Ella Fitzgerald and Louis Armstrong—a great team on a Verve album.

Above: Ella Fitzgerald on a Pablo album.

FATS WALLER

F ATS Waller was Thomas before he was Fats. He was born in Harlem in 1904. His father, Edward Martin Waller, was pastor of the Abyssinian Baptist Church, one of the country's most important black churches. His mother, Adaline Lockett Waller, was a pianist, organist, and vocalist. His grandfather, Adolph Waller, had been a violinist.

Music and religion became the keystones of Waller's life as a child. His parents were devout, religious, and musical, and so were their twelve children, of whom he was clearly the most talented. It was a matter of course that he studied the Bible, and at age six, he also began to learn the piano. He played in church and at prayer meetings and in his school orchestra. As he got older, he became increasingly fascinated by the world of ragtime and jazz—music, his father said, from "the devil's workshop."

W ALLER wanted to play both the devil's music and God's—ragtime and Bach chorales—depending on the mood he was in and the company he was with. But as he became more and more successful and better known playing music from the devil's workshop, it became increasingly difficult for him to play the other music he loved, the church music and the classics. He continued studying, though, with Carl Bohn and Leopold Godowsky. That music became his private sound—though he did, during the last years of his life, make some records playing the Hammond organ, giving it a swingingly tranquil sound. (His first recordings had used a pipe organ.)

T HE first organ Waller ever played was in his father's church. He graduated from that to the ten-thousand-dollar Wurlitzer at the Lincoln Theater, Harlem's famous movie house. At fourteen he was the stand-in for the regular organist. At fifteen he had dropped out of school to work as a pianist with a vaudeville troupe. In Boston with the group, he wrote a tune called "Boston Blues"; the title was later changed to "Squeeze Me." He had written his first hit, and he wasn't even sixteen.

Back in New York, Waller became the regular organist at the Lincoln Theater. The audiences loved his music and his improvised—and very funny—comments. James P. Johnson heard him at the Lincoln and took Waller under his wing.

Johnson was dean of the Harlem pianists, the "stride" giants like Willie "the Lion" Smith and Eubie Blake. Stride's roots are ragtime and the blues, but it also has a touch of Broadway and a great deal of rollicking, joyous spirit. The strong beat of the left hand—the stride—is its hallmark. Duke Ellington idolized Willie the Lion; Count Basie was another stride disciple who later used a leaner style and made more of less. From James P. Johnson, the father of stride, Waller was also able to learn about the delicacy of the right hand, for phrasing and excitement, and, as he used it, for humor and grace. "I taught him how to groove," said Johnson later about Waller, "how to make it sweet—the strong bass he had dates from that time. He stuck pretty well to my pattern, developed a lovely singing tone, a large melodic expression, and," Johnson finished, "being the son of a preacher, he had fervor."

Johnson got Waller his first jazz work, creating piano rolls, accompanying blues singers, and making the rounds of Harlem's rent parties. Originally "parlor socials" were held to raise money for the church. Later these fund-raisers made it possible to pay the rent. There was an admission charge and, in exchange, a platter of food and some great music. Prime attractions, piano players played everything: ragtime, jazz, blues, stride, and boogie woogie (long before anybody called it that).

During the mid-1920s, another side of the Fats Waller career began to develop in earnest, that of composer. He

A famous Fats Waller pose from an RCA publicity photograph. "One never knows, do one?"

wrote over four hundred songs in his short life, and many are still sung today.

IN 1928, Waller was playing at a club called Connie's Inn, a nightspot that was the famed Cotton Club's only competition in Harlem. (The Cotton Club's owner had gang connections, and other emerging clubs had a tendency to be squashed as they arose. The owners of Connie's Inn seemed to have had some kind of "arrangement" with somebody who mattered—the club flourished.) Waller had been playing at Connie's on and off and had contributed material for the club's elaborate shows with his partner, lyricist Andy Razaf.

RAZAF's real name was Andrea Menentania Razafinkeriefo; he was a nephew of Queen Ranavalona III of Madagascar. A remarkably good lyricist, Razaf and Waller wrote some great songs together. Two of them were for a new show at Connie's, to be called Hot Chocolates: "Ain't Misbehavin' " (Waller's 1929 recording is now in the National Academy of Recording Arts and Sciences Hall of Fame) and "Black and Blue."

Hot Chocolates was a hit, and the owners of Connie's decided to expand it and move it to Broadway. It opened on one of the hottest nights of the year, in June of 1928, and it became one of the hottest shows of the year. Among the bit players was Louis Armstrong, who sat in the pit and sang

Handful of Keys, a 1957 RCA offering.

"Ain't Misbehavin' " as a reprise between acts. The New York Times review closed by saying, "One song, a synthetic but entirely pleasant jazz ballad called 'Ain't Misbehavin' stands out, and its rendition between the acts by an unnamed member of the orchestra

was a highlight of the premiere."

ARMSTRONG's role expanded during the run of the show— eventually he sang "Ain't Misbehavin' " on stage, and he also did a number with Edith Wilson and Waller that was called "A Thousand Pounds of Rhythm." The show was a turning point of sorts for both Armstrong and Waller—Armstrong because he received such enormous popular success, and Waller because he decided that if Armstrong, with his growly voice, could succeed as a singer, then he could, too.

Razaf and Waller wrote many songs together; "Honeysuckle Rose" is another of their classics. But whatever Waller played or sang—and he made about five hundred records and copyrighted over four hundred compositions— he gave it the sound of joy, the sound of love, the easy—and most difficult—sound of heart and soul.

WALLER was an irrepressible blend of the secular and the devotional; he was an apostle of joy. Other pianists may have been better technicians, but nobody else combined his clarity, verve, easy grace, and rollicking rhythm. He was a clown at the piano with his famous trademark phrase, "One never knows, do one?" And he was an artist.

WALLER'S enthusiasm for life was translated into his eating habits, too. He was juicy. Very chubby. Plump. Fat, in fact—he weighed about three hundred pounds. He loved good food, good whiskey, good times. He was capable of eating nearly two dozen eggs with bacon for breakfast and as many hamburgers for lunch. Maybe he was cramming it in because he sensed it was all due to end too soon. Waller was only thirty-nine when he died. He was on a train coming back from California, where he'd made films and been in residence at the Zanzibar Club, to New York. He died of pneumonia in December 1943. He was on the Santa Fe *Chief*, just outside of Union Station in Kansas City, Missouri.

EARL HINES

THE piano has always occupied a special place in jazz. Its ability to sound like an orchestra establishes this pre-eminence: not only do piano riffs fill the largest gaps in many jazz arrangements, but they enable and inspire the player to construct solo works for the instrument which broaden its ensemble role. Except for the guitar, the piano performs this service uniquely in jazz, much as it has always done for popular and classical music.

NO one embodied this double role, soloist and bandleader, more creatively than Earl Kenneth Hines. Born to a musical family on December 28, 1903, in Pittsburgh, Hines began piano studies at the age of nine and went on to major in music at Schenley High School. His sister led her own band in the 1930s; their mother was an organist, and their father played cornet in local brass bands. Hines began working with a trio in his late teens, then joined a band led by singer Lois Deppe, touring with her in 1922. When Deppe organized the Pittsburgh Serenaders, Hines led them at the city's Lieder House. Later, after work with Harry Collins's orchestra, he went to Chicago to play at the Entertainer's Club.

THE windy city had been King Oliver's home since 1919. A few months before Earl Hines's arrival, Oliver had sent for Louis Armstrong to join him as second cornet in his band. Hines's apprenticeship there was at the Entertainer's Club with Carroll Dickerson, with whom he toured for almost a year on the Pantages vaudeville circuit, and with Erskine Tate's band. By 1925, Armstrong was on his own; two years later he hired Hines as music director of his orchestra, the Stompers, at the Sunset Café. (Armstrong preferred a "younger set" to King Oliver's group,

Earl Hines and his "Big Band" on a Golden Era album.

according to Hines). He replaced Lil Armstrong, Louis's wife, as pianist early in 1928.

THE association with Armstrong was an important career move. Not only did Hines play, arrange, and tour with the leading jazz figure of the day, but he even entered into a club-owning arrangement with him and drummer Zutty Singleton at Warwick Hall. The other great jazz figure in Chicago then was clarinetist Jimmie Noone; Hines started working with Noone's band late in

1927, while still continuing to record with Armstrong's hot groups for the Okeh label throughout 1928. On December 28, Earl Hines's twenty-fifth birthday, the pianist opened at Chicago's famed Grand Terrace Ballroom with his orchestra. A new era, his own, had started. Hines has rightly been called the father of modern jazz piano. His so-called "trumpet" style, with right-hand playing that paralleled the phrasing of Louis Armstrong's cornet solos, was virtuoso in character. His unorthodox left-hand rhythmic patterns permitted far more improvisation than stride and other keyboard styles had done. Hines influenced an entire generation of swing pianists in the 1930s and '40s: the nickname "Fatha" that adhered to him during these years was richly earned.

EARL Hines and his orchestra's first recording sessions took place on February 13 and 15, 1929, in Chicago—for the Victor Talking Machine Company, which that year would become RCA

Victor. Trombonist William Franklin vocalized on "Sweet Ella May" and "Good Little Bad Little You," while Hines handled the lyrics on "Sister Kate" and "Everybody Loves My Baby."

THE Grand Terrace was Hines's main base for ten years, during which time he freelanced often with other musicians. His band, meanwhile, was to become a breeding ground for many modern performers like Dizzy Gillespie, Charlie Parker, and Billy Eckstine. From July 1939 through March 1942, Hines recorded for the Victor Bluebird label hits such as "Stormy Monday," "Rosetta" (his best-known composition), "Boogie Woogie on St. Louis Blues," and "Jelly, Jelly"—with Eckstine as vocalist.

HOLLYWOOD was home for the Earl Hines orchestra until 1947. During this time bebop was born: with Gillespie, Parker, and Sarah Vaughan in the 1942–43 band, it may fairly be said that this was where it all started. The first bebop anthem, "Night in Tunisia," was recorded

by them, though mainstream ballads like Billy Eckstine's "Skylark" were also cut by this astonishingly versatile group. When Eckstine left for a solo career, Hines experimented with an all-female string section, performing semisymphonic works. But the days of big bands were numbered: in 1948, Hines disbanded his and, in a move of his-

A Bandstand Records album of the Earl Hines Orchestra featuring Billy Eckstine.

toric proportions, joined Louis Armstrong's All Stars, playing with them until 1951.

LATE in that year, he began performing with a variety of small groups, starting with his own sextet. The Hangover Club in San Francisco, where Hines first played in 1952, became his base

after 1955. Late in 1957, he co-directed a band in Europe with trombonist Jack Teagarden. In 1960, Hines moved with his family to Oakland, California, where, after continued touring and recording, he opened his own club in 1963. Solo albums, such as *Earl Hines at Home* (Contact, 1964) and a combo-backed, nostalgic *Up to Date* (Victor, 1965), kept his name before the public, as did repeated trips to Europe (including a 1966 U.S. government-sponsored tour of Russia). He was featured in a "Swinging Era" package during 1967 and appeared at London's Jazz Expo the following year.

HINES'S expanded schedule included tours of Europe, Japan, and Australia during the 1970s and a landmark series of albums, *Hines Plays Duke Ellington, 1971–75*. His personality, like his playing, remained enthusiastic and happy throughout his career; he was in demand everywhere, performing even through the weekend before his death in Oakland on April 22, 1983.

MILES DAVIS

MILES *Ahead.* That's a Miles Davis album that came out in 1957. It's also where Miles Davis always was. The headline on his *New York Times* obituary put it this way: "Jazz Genius. Defined Cool."

Davis's life began in prosperous obscurity. In 1926, he was born Miles Dewey Davis III, in Alton, Illinois, just north of St. Louis, the son of a dental surgeon. His mother had been a music teacher before her marriage; she played the organ, piano, and violin.

DAVIS traced his musical roots to two things: listening to a radio show called "Harlem Rhythms" when he was seven or eight, and when he was even younger, walking to and from church on Saturday nights from his grandfather's farm in Arkansas and hearing, in the dark on the country road, someone playing the guitar and singing. "That kind of sound in music, that blues, church, back-road funk kind of thing, that southern, midwestern, rural sound and rhythm. I think it started getting into my blood on them spook-filled Arkansas back-roads after dark when the owls came out hooting. So when I started taking music lessons I might have already had some idea of what I wanted my music to sound like."

WHEN Davis was twelve, he started trumpet lessons on an old trumpet his uncle had given him. At summer camp he was allowed to play taps and reveille. His mother objected when he got a new trumpet for his thirteenth birthday; she wanted him to play the violin. He began to work professionally on weekends while still in high school.

In 1944, Billy Eckstine's band came to St. Louis. Davis later wrote that he

> . . .just picked up my trumpet and went on over to see if I could catch something. . . . The first thing I see when I got inside was this man running up to me, asking if I was a trumpet player. . . . So the guy said, "Come on, we need a trumpet player. Our trumpet got sick." This guy takes me up on the bandstand and puts the music in front of me. . . .

A woodcut of Miles Davis (left) and John Coltrane, by Esther Mueller. Courtesy of Ned Moran, Hudson Valley Rock and Roll Museum of Art.

> That guy who ran up to me was Dizzy. I didn't recognize him at first. But soon as he started playing, I knew who he was. . . . I couldn't even read the music—don't even talk about playing—for listening to Bird and Diz.

Bird—Charlie Parker—on alto saxophone, Dizzy Gillespie on trumpet, Sarah Vaughan singing, and Billy Eckstine: in musical terms, that was a revolutionary band. Davis played with them for two weeks.

That first night changed Davis's life. He decided "right then and there" to come to New York, where all these musicians came from. And when he got to the Big Apple to attend the Juilliard School of Music, Dizzy took him under his wing, and Charlie Parker became his roommate. Soon he was playing in Parker's combo on 52nd Street.

"I've come close to matching the feeling of that night in 1944 in my music," Davis wrote in his autobiography in 1989,

> . . .but I've never quite got there. I've gotten close, but not all the way there. I'm always looking for it, listening and feeling for it, though, trying to always feel it in and through the music I play every day. I still remember when I was just a kid, still wet behind the ears, hanging out with all these great musicians, my idols even until this day. Sucking in everything. Man, it was something.

47

So was Davis. He was the most famous trumpeter of his generation and took his place in the line of great trumpeters from Louis Armstrong to Dizzy Gillespie to Wynton Marsalis. His music became a jazz touchstone for four decades, a model for generations of jazz musicians.

There was a Miles sound, but never a Miles style, because he was always evolving, always innovating, always changing. His style included the blues—the sound of

Miles Davis with Stan Getz (left) in 1951. Courtesy of the Frank Driggs Collection.caption

that country road—but there was more: jazz, bepop, cool jazz, pop, flamenco, modal playing, free-form improvisation, classical music, rock, funk, Indian music, Arab music, African music. He played with the best musicians, hiring young men and letting them be their best, and they moved on to innovations of their own. His collaborations inspired those he played with; he, in turn, was inspired by them. Arranger Gil Evans was his best friend, in music and in life. It was Evans who wrote the classic "Boplicity." Davis made dozens and dozens of records with other people and with his own groups.

He was inducted into the Knights of Malta (making him Sir Miles) in 1988. In 1984, he received the Sonning Award for lifetime

achievement in music, and in 1990, he won his 24th Grammy, this time for lifetime achievement in music.

Many people called Davis arrogant. Much of what seemed like arrogance was sometimes pride, sometimes outrage at America's spoken and silent racism, sometimes just honesty. At one point in his career, he turned his back on audiences as he played and walked offstage when he was not soloing. The music was what was important, not who was playing it or where he was standing.

In the years of Davis's heroin addiction during the early fifties, his life and and his career fell apart. He quit twice—cold turkey each time, but later heavily used cocaine and other drugs. Davis also had recurring medical problems. In 1957, he had a throat operation to remove nodes from his vocal cords; two days later, he lost his temper and shouted at someone "who was trying to convince me to go into a deal I didn't want." His voice was permanently damaged; from then on, he spoke in a raspy whisper. In 1975, he retired from music— "my silence," he called it. He had diabetes, ulcers, throat nodes, hip surgery, and bursitis.

IN 1981, he returned with a new album and a new band. In 1989, he died of pneumonia, respiratory failure, and a stroke.

Davis usually didn't like what people wrote about him.

> I never thought there was nothing nobody could say about an album of mine. I just want everyone to listen to the music, and make up their own minds. I never did like no one writing about what I played on an album, trying to explain what I was trying to do. The music speaks for itself.

Davis never heard what the Reverend Jesse Jackson, one of the speakers at his memorial service, called his sound—"eternal music that elevated feeling into art and song into prayer. He was our music man, leaning back, blowing out of his horn, out of his soul, all the beauty and pain and sadness and determination and wishful longing of our own lives.

He would growl his independence and ours out of his horn. And sometimes by turning his back as he played a solitary song, he would only let us hear him talking to God."

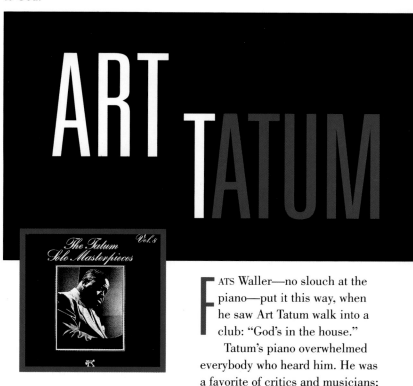

ART TATUM

FATS Waller—no slouch at the piano—put it this way, when he saw Art Tatum walk into a club: "God's in the house."

Tatum's piano overwhelmed everybody who heard him. He was a favorite of critics and musicians; many considered him the greatest pianist in jazz history. A complete master of the instrument, a virtuoso, with unparalleled technique, ease, and speed on the keys coupled with flowing ideas and great finesse, he was a genius of the piano.

ATUM was also nearly blind. Born with cataracts on both his eyes, despite undergoing several operations during his childhood, he remained with only par-

Art Tatum at the piano in London, 1938. Courtesy of the Frank Driggs Collection.

tial vision in one eye.

Born in Toledo, Ohio, in 1910, Tatum was the son of amateur musicians: his father played the guitar and his mother, the piano. He learned to play the piano as a child; at the Cousino School for the Blind in Columbus, he also played guitar, violin, and accordion. Spending two years at the Toledo School of Music, he began working in clubs in and around Toledo, forming his own group, and in 1929 he became the pianist in residence at radio station WSPD.

ATUM went to New York City in 1932 to accompany vocalist Adelaide Hall, and at the same time, he began filling in at New York clubs. For the next several years, he played at various nightspots around the country—the Three Deuces in Chicago, the Paramount and Club Alabam in Hollywood. He made his first European tour in 1938 and came back to play in California and at New York's famous Café Society Downtown.

Tatum's first trio, in 1943, included Tiny Grimes and Slam

Stewart. In 1945, he began the first of his annual concert tours, becoming a prolific recording artist, from his first piano solos in 1933 to his last sessions a few weeks before his death in 1956. Two of his discs, "Body and Soul" and "Tea for Two," made it to the pop charts. "Tea for Two," recorded in 1939, was also selected for the National Academy of Record-ing Arts and Sciences Hall of Fame.

In the last eighteen months of his life, Tatum worked mostly as a concert artist. His last performance took place at the Hollywood Bowl on August 15, 1956, with nineteen thousand people in the audience. He started a national concert tour after that, but he was already ill with uremia and had to return to Los Angeles, where he died on November 5, 1956.

AZZ critic Leonard Feather said that Tatum was the first jazz pianist with complete technical command: "His brain and fingers moved so quickly that he expressed in one measure more ideas, more subtleties of phrasing and dynamics and harmony, than could most of his predecessors in four. Graced by Tatum's gossamer touch and articulation, the keys became feathers. Every style known to keyboard jazz was at his command." Tatum was the consummate musician, the piano player's piano player. He wasn't like anyone else; he couldn't be compared to any other musicians; he was simply Art Tatum, in a class by himself—the best.

SARAH VAUGHAN

BILLIE Holiday had the pain; Ella Fitzgerald, the purity and the laughter; Lena Horne, the cool. Sarah Vaughan—one of the last of the great jazz divas—had the sass. She also had the range—a spread nothing short of extraordinary, from her lowest notes, almost a male baritone, to her cool soprano high notes. Born in Newark, New Jersey, in 1924, Sarah Vaughan also had the musical background. Her father, a professional carpenter, was a talented guitarist. Her mother sang in the choir at Mount Zion Baptist Church.

VAUGHAN started studying piano when she was seven and was a vocal soloist and church organist by the time she was twelve. She sang at parties and played the piano at Newark Arts High School. Her piano playing was one of the first of several instrumental influences on her singing: "While I was playing piano in the school band," she

Sarah Vaughan at the piano. With her are Duke Ellington (left) and Billy Eckstine. Photograph by Popsie Randolph courtesy of the Frank Driggs Collection.

told a *Down Beat* interviewer, "I learned to take music apart and analyze the notes and put it back together again. By doing this, I learned to sing differently from all the other singers."

At nineteen, Vaughan won an Amateur Night competition at the Apollo "on a dare," she said later, "from some friends in New Jersey." She sang "Body and Soul," and she was a sensation. Ella Fitzgerald had won an Apollo Amateur Night contest a decade earlier; now she cautioned Vaughan about agents and managers. Billy Eckstine, who was to be a longtime friend, heard Vaughan and recommended her to Earl Hines as covocalist for his big band.

HINES hired Vaughan not only as vocalist with Eckstine, but also as second pianist, and within weeks she was playing in the same band as many of her idols. She met Charlie Parker and Dizzy Gillespie in the Hines band: "I think their playing influenced my singing," she said in

another *Down Beat* story. "Horns always influenced me more than voices. . . . as soon as I hear an arrangement, I get ideas, kind of like blowing a horn. I guess I never sing a tune the same way twice."

WHEN Billy Eckstine left the Hines band in 1944 to form his own modern jazz group, Vaughan went with him to join such top-notch musicians as Dizzy Gillespie, Miles Davis, Fats Navarro, Charlie Parker, and Art Blakey. She was the perfect vocal counterpart for their innovative jazz work. Her voice was amazingly supple, her pitch true; she was a willing and athletic improviser; and her harmonic sense was both instinctive and schooled. She was the voice of the new jazz era.

"Sassy" was, with Ella Fitzgerald, one of the great scat singers. Jazz scatting formally began when Louis Armstrong used some nonsense syllables to cover lyrics he'd forgotten, and his audience loved it. Scat draws a straight line between the singer and the instrumentalists, because it allows the vocalist to use his or her voice like an instrument. It has to be balanced by good lyric singing to be at its best, and Vaughan refined the mix to perfection. Her voice was always instrumental; scat gave her the chance to fully explore the possibilities of her vocal ability.

Sarah Vaughan with Stan Kenton (left) and Nat "King" Cole in 1951. Courtesy of the Frank Driggs Collection.

VAUGHAN made her debut record with the Eckstine band in 1944, singing "I'll Wait and Pray." By the end of the year, she was recording successfully on her own, and aside from a short stint as vocalist with John Kirby in 1945–46, she stayed a solo artist for the rest of her career.

"The Divine One," as she came to be known, bridged two eras—from jazz and swing to popular music, prerock, and from the age of the big band, with its girl or boy singer as a mere accessory, to the contemporary era of solo singing stardom.

THE history of music—popular as well as classical—is written in a succession of styles. The twentieth century began with a dance boom, and its music was ragtime. The rags blended into jazz, and its free spirit blended into the careful arrangements of swing. Swing lasted through World War II; the end of the war was the end of the big-band era. The war had driven up band prices—players were scarce. The government paid for music to entertain the troops, but after the war, club owners couldn't afford the tab.

EVEN more, popular taste was changing: singers were emerging as first-rank stars. Bing Crosby was the earliest. He was a jazz singer first, in the twenties, and by the midthirties, he was a popular star on his own, in movies and on the radio. But most singers had the spotlight only when they were in front of the band; bandleaders were the big stars. Frank Sinatra was the key figure in the change—thrilling bobby-soxers by the thousands in front of the Dorsey band at New York's Paramount Theater. And by the end of the war, club and theater owners had realized that a singer backed by a small instrumental group was a lot more affordable than a big band with name soloists and a star on the bandstand beating time.

At the same time, bebop was evolving from jazz and swing, and

53

modern cool jazz grew out of bop. Until Elvis Presley and the Beatles and rock and roll, jazz remained a substantial part of the music market. Dave Brubeck, Chet Baker, Stan Kenton, Miles Davis, John Coltrane, Sarah Vaughan—these were the jazz names of the new era. Vaughan sang jazz; she also sang middle-of-the-road pop ballads.

"Tenderly" was her first hit on the pop charts, in 1947. She was "accompanied by" (not "singing with") George Treadwell's Orchestra. "Nature Boy," "It's Magic," "That Lucky Old Sun" are just some of her pop and jazz hits. And of course "Poor Butterfly," almost a signature song.

SARAH Vaughan's legacy is unmatchable: fluent phrasing, impeccable tone, incredible range, marvelous inventiveness, exemplary musicianship. Vaughan died in 1990, one of the last of the jazz era, a great singer, a great stylist. Sassy, they called her. And divine.

COUNT BASIE

ENDURANCE is a prized asset in the world of music. For musicians who, like Mozart and Schubert, died young or those who, like Count Basie, were still active at eighty, the secret has been to keep creating—to immerse themselves in, and perfect, their art. The secret transcends time and boundary, spanning centuries, continents, and cultures.

William Basie was born August 21, 1904, in Red Bank, New Jersey. As a youngster he took piano lessons from his mother but made his public debut as a drummer. The influence of Willie "the Lion" Smith and Fats Waller—and the offer of tuition money from Waller—prompted Basie to focus on the piano. He began working summers in Asbury Park, New Jersey, then at various clubs in New York, including a spell with Elmer Snowden's band. He toured widely as a piano and organ accompanist to vaudeville performers. After two years on the Keith Orpheum Circuit with Sonny Thompson's band and the Gonzelle White show, Basie fell seriously ill and left the circuit in Kansas City.

AFTER recovering, Basie began to play for the Whitman Sisters and to work in local theaters. His experience as a blues accompanist led to his first real break the following year, when he was summoned to Dallas to join Walter Page's Blue Devils, a Kansas City-based touring band whose vocalist was Jimmy Rushing. He performed with Walter and trumpeter Oran "Hot Lips" Page for a year, then joined Bennie Moten's

Kansas City Orchestra.

MOTEN was a Victor recording artist with a national following; he gave up his own piano spot to Basie so that he could direct the band. Trombonist-guitarist-arranger Eddie Durham joined at the same time, and the first Victor session with the new members took place on October 23, 1929, in Chicago. Soon Rushing and Lips Page defected to the Moten organization, and a dynasty was born.

Count Basie honed his skills brilliantly with the likes of tenor saxophonist Ben Webster, clarinetist-altoist Harlan Leonard, and trumpeter Booker Washington before leaving the orchestra in 1934 to try his hand at band-leading, under Moten's auspices, in Little Rock. Then Bennie Moten's sudden death in 1935 changed things for everyone.

THE main band broke up, but Basie and pianist Ira "Buster" Moten (Bennie's nephew) organized a nine-piece group that performed on Kansas City station W9XBY from its home base, the Reno Club. It was during this

engagement that Bill Basie was dubbed "Count" by a radio announcer who thought he belonged with the royalty of Duke Ellington and Earl Hines, among others. Nor were just the locals impressed: when A&R recording genius John Hammond heard Basie's broadcasts on his car radio in New York, he brought the band to the immediate attention of Benny Goodman, who arranged a contract for the band—now called Count Basie and his Orchestra—with Decca Records the following year.

BY this time, Basie had brought together such powerful soloists as trumpeter Buck Clayton and tenor saxophonist Lester Young. With them he defined the truly modern style of a beat-oriented ensemble, with subtle and innovative piano riffs, commercial blues, and a driving spontaneity that became the envy of every other band in America. The bands of Goodman, Artie Shaw, and Charlie Barnet were powerfully influenced by Basie's style and level of performance, as were numerous other bands that came together under the sonic umbrella of swing. By early 1938, with successes at New York's Savoy ballroom and Famous Door club, Count Basie's fame had become international, his orchestra and repertoire legendary.

BESIDES Rushing and Basie himself, the vocals featured Billie Holiday and Helen Humes, and though phenomenally successful with head arrangements during most of its formative years, the band eventually acquired the orchestration skills of Andy Gibson. The band signed with Columbia Records in November 1939 (a few months after Benny Goodman did the same) and stayed through 1946, registering many chart hits: "All of Me," "Jimmy's Blues" (with Rushing), "The Mad Boogie," and "Blue Skies" among them. But these were eclipsed by the RCA Victor sides Basie cut, starting with the number-one smash "Open the Door, Richard" (vocals by Harry Edison and Bill Johnson) in February 1947. It was a true pop sensation.

Much had changed during

the World War II years. Big bands had reached their economic and expressive peaks, in swing terms anyway. Bebop and related smaller-group forms became the rage, and although progressive bands like Stan Kenton's and Woody Herman's had hits beyond the period, most traditional ensembles gave way to the age of the vocal-

ist—band singers, mostly, who now fronted pickup groups led by arranger-conductors. Of all the bands who played on, undiminished, throughout the 1940s, Count Basie's Orchestra stands out—alive, evolving, and in demand.

The band spent much of its time in California during these

years. They appeared in movies—four in 1943 alone: *Crazy House, Reveille with Beverly, Hit Parade of 1943*, and the memorable *Stage Door Canteen*. The train of Victor singles continued with "Free Eats," "One O'Clock Boogie" (issued almost simultaneously with a Decca reissue of Basie's 1937 theme song hit "One O'Clock Jump"), and "I Ain't Mad at You" in 1947. Many of the band's instrumental sides—"Rat Race," "Seventh Avenue Express," "Basie's Basement"—didn't make the charts but have been reissued frequently over the years as album compilations became a preferred medium of listening to jazz.

IN 1950, Count Basie disbanded the Orchestra and organized a small group featuring saxophonist Wardell Gray, clarinetist Buddy DeFranco and trumpeter Clark Terry. With arrangers Neal Hefti and Johnny Mandel he eventually relaunched the big band with new, swinging blues and jazz originals by Hefti, Ernie Wilkens, and Quincy Jones. The band toured Scandinavia in 1954 and Europe in 1956 and made its first tour of Great Britain in 1957. Tenor saxophonist Eddie "Lockjaw" Davis and trumpeter Joe Newman had starring roles, along with previous band regulars—including guitarist Freddy Green, who lasted with Basie well into the 1970s. The band appeared overseas on a regular basis, making its first tour of Japan in 1963.

UNTIL his death on April 26, 1984, Count Basie was never out of the public's consciousness. He took part in many studio collaborations—with Frank Sinatra, Ella Fitzgerald, Sammy Davis Jr., Tony Bennett, and others. His films continued unabated and included *Cinderfella, Sex and the Single Girl, Jamboree, Man of the Family,* and *One More Time.* His legacy, however, is the skillful traversal of mainstream jazz that he made his own during the early 1930s and which endured for half a century.

SONNY ROLLINS

PROBABLY the most influential tenor saxophonist of the post-fifties jazz era, aside from John Coltrane, is Sonny Rollins. Theodore Walter Rollins was born in New York City in 1929. His brother played violin, and his sister was a church pianist, but his strongest influences were the Coleman Hawkins and Charlie Parker schools of jazz. He grew up in the same neighborhood as Hawkins, Thelonious Monk, and Bud Powell, hearing bebop as it, too, grew up.

ROLLINS was eighteen years old when he cut his first record with Babs Gonzales. At nineteen he recorded with Bud Powell and Fats Navarro. In 1950, he left New York for Chicago where he studied with drummer Ike Day, believing that working with a percussionist would improve his rhythmic ideas for the saxophone. This is the first, brief indication of a pattern that is a Rollins hallmark: withdrawal from the jazz scene in order to concentrate on

An RCA publicity photograph of Sonny Rollins.

the evolution of his playing.

I N 1951, Rollins cut his first record with Miles Davis and also his first with his own group. Over the next three years, he recorded with Miles again, and with Charlie Parker, Thelonious Monk, Max Roach, and the Modern Jazz Quartet. He also composed three of his best-known jazz works: "Oleo," "Doxy," and "Airegin."

T HE title "Airegin" sounds like it refers to carbonated booze or very hip sneakers, but spelled backwards it's actually a country in Africa. All three tunes were featured on *Bags' Groove*, a Miles Davis album that was subtitled "Miles Davis and the Modern Jazz Giants." In addition to Rollins and Davis, it featured Milt Jackson on vibes, Thelonius Monk and Horace Silver on piano, and Kenny Clarke on drums.

R OLLINS joined the Max Roach-Clifford Brown Quintet in 1955 and with this group made some of his most significant contributions to jazz. His "Valse Hot" was followed by a rush of three-quarter-time numbers by other musicians, all leading to the exploration of the rhythmic possibilities of a variety of meters in jazz.

ROLLINS was gone to Chicago again in 1954 to work as a day laborer. His second, best-known silent time was from August 1959 to November 1961—this time in New York, incognito and given to practicing at night on the pedestrian walkway of the Williamsburg Bridge, high over the East River. The RCA album *The Bridge* marked his return, but from 1963 to 1965, there was another voluntary retirement. This time Rollins travelled to India and Japan. From 1967 to 1972, in ill health, he withdrew again, coming back to record *Sonny Rollins's Next Album* and play in public once more. His self-imposed exiles involved extreme self-criticism, reassessment of his personal and musical values, intense practice on his instrument, and exploration first of Rosicrucianism and later of yoga.

Rollins's style, as it evolved, maintained his bebop roots with lengthy, free-association solos based on music from many sources. In 1972, he was awarded a Guggenheim Fellowship for his contributions to modern music. His "Concerto for Saxophone and Orchestra" was first heard in Japan with the Yomiuri Nippon Symphony Orchestra in 1985. He also wrote the score for the film *Alfie*. The soundtrack album, released in 1965, was probably his most commercially successful release.

SONNY Rollins made jazz history for his music and his introspection. The repeated disappearances and the exciting reappearances were flamboyant because they were extreme and because they were in a style unusual for jazz: an intense, directed, removed, and personal evolution of a man and his music.

With Miles Davis and Thelonius Monk, Sonny Rollins was the kind of musician who led the way, more interested in the next sound than the last. There are many jazz musicians who have taken their cue from Preservation Hall—think of the big-band sound of the Glenn Miller Orchestra, dipped in brass, sounding

the same for over fifty years since the death of Glenn Miller in 1944. Others have chosen to evolve, to take risks, to grow, and to change. That path, in any field, is never well travelled and is certainly never the shortest distance between two points, but the one who takes it is frequently worth following.

Sonny Rollins's album The Quartets, RCA.

DAVE BRUBECK

DAVE Brubeck is another jazz star whose first training was in classical music. In 1921, he was born in Concord, California, a small town approximately thirty miles outside of San Francisco. His father managed cattle ranches; his mother was the daughter of a stagecoach operator whose run went from Concord to Oakland. She was also a musician. The family lived in Concord until Dave was eight years old, and he later said the family house "was built for music. Pianos were in four different rooms there, and they were going all day long. My mother was teaching, or my brothers were practicing." Music, he said, was the first thing he heard in the morning, and the last thing he heard at night, "and we didn't even have a radio."

BRUBECK'S mother gave him his first piano lessons. Later, he said, "It was apparent right from the beginning that I would be a composer." He started improvising when he was four years old. When he was six, he and a friend formed a tap-dance-ukelele-piano team and performed for local groups like the Lions Club. For all that, he wasn't a good student; he refused to study and played everything by ear. His mother didn't insist, but she did give him lots of theory, ear training, and harmony. Throughout high school, he worked with bands in the California mountain country.

HE didn't hear a great deal of jazz. Occasionally, he said later, he listened to the "Benny Goodman Show" on Saturday nights, hearing recordings of Teddy Wilson, Duke Ellington, and Fats Waller.

As to records, I had only this one Fats Waller record, which I still have. I bought it in Sacramento when I was about fourteen. It was "Honey on the Moon Tonight" and "Close as Fingers in a Glove."

I used to dream about maybe Benny Goodman was going to come down this road. All day

Brubeck at the 1971 Newport Jazz Festival in New York. Photograph by Jack Vartoogian.

I'd dream, as we drove the cattle, about how Goodman would have to come through the cattle—going from Stockton to Sacramento for a one-nighter, and I wouldn't let him through unless he'd let me on the band bus, and there'd bound to be a piano on the bus and everybody'd be jamming and somebody would get to hear me play!

YEARS later, when Brubeck was working at a small club in San Francisco, Goodman did come to hear him; Brubeck said he was so nervous, he stopped playing. (The singer was so awed, he left out two bars of "Body and Soul.")

AT Mills College, where Brubeck earned a masters degree, he studied with composer Darius Milhaud. Eventually, he himself was a teacher at the University of California. That might be part of the reason he had such a lock on the college market in the fifties and sixties. Brubeck

also won first place in the piano division of the *Playboy* poll every year from 1961 to 1966, and the Dave Brubeck Quartet placed first or second in the *Down Beat* readers' poll for a solid ten years.

The Quartet was formed in 1951. It grew out of earlier groups Brubeck had formed, notably an octet that recorded for Fantasy Records in 1946, not long after Brubeck returned from military service during World War II. The initial Quartet included Paul Desmond, whose alto sax was ever-so-cool, stretching and curving sound, Gene Wright on bass, and Joe Morello on drums.

THE Quartet was chamber jazz—a kind of classicized jazz. Their sound contained the harmonics of Bartok, the dignity of Bach, and the romanticism of Rachmaninoff—as well as Brubeck's debt to Tatum, Ellington, and Waller. The Quartet was a tight ensemble; the counterpoint of Desmond's alto and Brubeck's piano was suave and rich and full of obvious rapport. It made jazz a concert attraction on campuses where before the only concert attraction had been dance music. Students tuned in to the Quartet's unusual time signatures, sophisticated sound, and coolness of bop with a classic twist. Some of the Quartet's signature albums were *Jazz Goes to College* and *Jazz Goes to Junior College.*

In 1959, the Brubeck Quartet and the New York Philharmonic under the baton of Leonard Bernstein joined forces for *Dialogue for Jazz Combo and Symphony*, composed by Dave's brother Howard. Later albums were made with his sons Chris, Darius, and Danny.

THE Quartet played at the White House in 1964 at the request of Lady Bird Johnson. King Hussein of Jordan was the guest of honor. In addition to the New York Philharmonic, the Quartet played with the Berlin Philharmonic, also in 1964. Brubeck has lectured on music at many colleges and universities. In 1961, he received an honorary doctorate from the University of the Pacific in recognition of his musical and humanitarian contributions.

The Quartet split in 1967,

and Brubeck worked with a variety of sidemen over the next decade, including clarinetist Bill Smith and baritone saxophonist Gerry Mulligan. He also worked as a soloist and a lecturer. The Quartet reunited before Brubeck's death in 1977, the same year that the *25th Anniversary Reunion* album, recorded by A & M Records, was released.

CRITICS have argued about Brubeck's playing—heavy-handed to some, romantic to others—but all agree that his solos could take flight and build into climactic excitement, that he did marvelously exciting things with time, and that he was an important influence in modern jazz.

Dave Brubeck on a Columbia album.

LENA Horne was always beautiful. Her beauty shows in a photograph of her as a two-year-old, holding a flower, in the October 1919 issue of the NAACP *Branch Bulletin.* The cheekbones haven't emerged from the baby fat yet, but she looks fiercely determined, a tiny bit scared, and as always, beautiful. She was so beautiful that she worried that she was valued for her looks and not her voice.

Horne was born into America's other aristocracy, the black elite. Horne is the great-great-great-granddaughter of slaves—the first, Sinai Reynolds, was a favored slave, a house servant who could read and write. Sinai was a first-generation American, born in Maryland; her mother had probably been brought here from Senegal. One of Reynold's children was taken from her and sent to colonize Liberia; two others, including her daughter Nellie, were sold. Nellie became the property of the wealthy and powerful Calhouns; her son Moses had spent half his life in slavery before the Civil War ended. He prospered, buying property and soon owning a grocery store and a restaurant, and his daughter Cora graduated from Atlanta University. She married Edwin Horn (the "e" was added later), son of an English adventurer and a Native American. Horn had several careers—journalist, writer, educator, and politician—and was successful in each. He and Cora moved north, settling in Brooklyn, then just changing from farmland to lovely small communities with broad streets and ample parks. They bought a brownstone, where they lived with their four sons—including Teddy, Lena's father.

TEDDY was the first family rascal, radiantly charming (with Lena's smile), handsome, devilish. He was born to money and liked having it; he just didn't like working. He loved parties, women, sports, good times. He married one of the most popular young women in his group, Edna Scottron.

LENA Mary Calhoun Horne was born on June 30, 1917. Her parents separated two years later. Teddy went west, Edna left to become an actress, and for seven years, Lena was her grandmother's child. Cora was deeply involved in several movements— the young NAACP, the fight for the vote for women—and belonged to the clubs of a prosperous woman's social life. Lena was taken to meetings, expected to behave, told to listen, and sometimes quizzed afterwards.

When she was seven, Horne's life changed radically. In effect her mother kidnapped her. She

Lena Horne, age two, in an NAACP bulletin.

took Lena south, and for the next decade, Lena alternated between Edna and Cora, north and south, at home in neither place. Children teased her in the south for her northern accent, in the north for her southern accent. In the south she was called "a little yellow bastard," and she played in the sun, hoping to darken her skin. In the north she was a child of scandal—divorced parents, mother on the stage. She was beaten by her mother, who was equally capable of sudden bursts of great affection. She was frightened of her mother,

who appeared and disappeared regularly, but she was awed by her beauty. She felt safe with her grandmother but was kept at a distance by her icy sternness. At least in Brooklyn she was a Horne, and there that mattered.

IN Brooklyn, Horne took lessons in music and drama. She sang "Indian Love Call" at every Junior Deb party in 1933; she studied at the Anna Jones Dancing School, and when the school won a week's engagement at the Harlem Opera House, she was one of the students performing an Isadora Duncan dance to "Stormy Weather," Harold Arlen's hit song. She had a starring role in the Junior Theater Guild of Brooklyn's annual charity show and won her first bravos.

THROUGH a friend of her mother's, Horne got a chance to audition for the Cotton Club's 1934 show. The Cotton Club was the most famous and lucrative speakeasy of them all. It was what jazz was about in the twenties, and in 1934, it still featured "tall, tan, and terrific showgirls." There were three shows a night, at 8:30

P.M., 11:30 P.M., and 2:00 A.M.; each show lasted two hours. At sixteen, Lena was the youngest performer at the club. She was chaperoned by her mother, who had turned into a classic stage mother, and friends of her father put out the word that she was to be "protected." Cab Calloway and the boys in the band called her "Brooklyn." She got $25 a week for three shows a night, seven days a week.

THE Cotton Club led to a series of other breaks. First was a part in a Broadway drama with music, *Dance with Your Gods*, about voodoo. Horne had a solo dance in one ballet, after which she took the subway uptown (no time to wait for the curtain calls) for the 11:30 P.M. show at the Cotton Club. Later she was a girl singer for Noble Sissle's Society Orchestra tour.

HORNE was offered her first film part in an all-black, quickie musical, *The Duke is Tops*, later released as *Black Venus*. She was one of the *Blackbirds of 1939* on Broadway, and the *New York Times* review mentioned her as a "radiantly beautiful sepia girl" and praised her singing. She toured with Charlie Barnet's band, made her first records with them, and appeared with the band at New York's Paramount Theater. From that came an offer from Café Society, one of the city's most successful nightclubs. Located in a Sheridan Square basement in Greenwich Village, with matchbooks that read, "The wrong place for the right people," Café Society was founded by a communist, Barney Josephson, but it was enormously popular with the mon-eyed, uptown crowd. Billie Holiday, Zero Mostel, Josh White, Comden and Green, and Judy Holliday all starred there—and Billie Holiday helped build Horne's confidence for the first show. She was paid $75 a week, and she was a hit.

IN 1941, Horne was offered a job at a new club in Los Angeles. It was to be called the Trocadero, and she was to be its first star. (When she couldn't decide whether or not to go, Duke Ellington told her she should let "the whole world benefit" from her "incredible radiance.") World War II changed the Trocadero plans; the club was now called Little Troc, but Horne was still the star, with new songs arranged for her by Billy Strayhorn, Duke's pianist and arranger. That performance led to an MGM contract and the lead in *Cabin in the Sky*. Lena Horne had arrived.

HORNE was just in time for NAACP negotiations with studio heads for guidelines on the depiction of blacks in films, the use of blacks as extras,

Lena Horne on the Audio Fidelity label.

Lena Horne at the Sands, recorded live at the Sands Hotel in Las Vegas, an RCA album.

and the integration of blacks into technical and crafts jobs. Horne's father was more direct in a meeting with MGM head L. B. Mayer. "I can hire a maid for her," Teddy said about Lena. "Why should she act one?"

THE contract was signed: Horne was to be paid $350 a week and guaranteed forty weeks per year and a $100-a-week raise each year for seven years. In her first screen test, the NAACP and L. B. Mayer notwithstanding, she was paired with Eddie "Rochester" Anderson, of Jack Benny fame, to test for the comic black servant love interest in a Jeanette MacDonald movie. Horne's face was smeared with dark makeup because they decided she wasn't black enough; Ethel Waters got the part. Hollywood eventually found a solution to Horne's light skin: Max Factor developed a coppery-caramel colored pancake makeup that made her skin look darker without making her look ridiculous.

HORNE was in fourteen movies, beginning with *Panama Hattie* in 1942 and ending with *Death of a Gunfighter* in 1969. She is best known for *Cabin in the Sky* and *Stormy Weather.*

There were also club dates and special appearances—at the Savoy Plaza (where Horne was the first black to headline, though no blacks could stay overnight at the hotel), the Capitol theater (co-starring with Duke Ellington, with people lined up around the block waiting to get in), and in night-clubs in America and in Europe. She made a series of records, hitting the charts with "Stormy Weather," "One for My Baby (And One More for the Road)," and "Deed I Do," among others.

IN 1947, Brooklyn held a Lena Horne Day. That same year she married Lennie Hayton, two-time Oscar winner for musical direction (for *On the Town* and *Singin' in the Rain*). Lennie was a classically trained musician, protegé of the great conductor Serge Koussevitzsky, who fell in love with jazz early in his life and became pianist for the Paul Whiteman Orchestra. (Other members of the orchestra included Bix Beiderbecke, Bunny Berigan, Frankie Trombauer, Jack Teagarden, Red Norvo, Tommy and Jimmy Dorsey, and a vocal trio whose lead baritone was Bing Crosby.) Hayton went on to conduct major radio show orchestras and then moved to Hollywood and film musicals.

Horne continued making movies and records, headlining in

Lena Horne, as beautiful as ever, at the 1993 JVC Jazz Festival, Lincoln Center's Avery Fisher Hall in Manhattan. A Jack Vartoogian photograph.

Las Vegas and appearing in New York, Paris, and London. In 1957, she starred again on Broadway in *Jamaica*, and in 1981 (at age 64), she opened in *Lena Horne: The Lady and Her Music*. It was her first appearance in nearly a decade. The critics compared her to Caruso, Pavlova, Nijinsky, George M. Cohan, Mary Martin, Frank Sinatra, Fred Astaire, and Charlie Parker. She was, in other words, the best. The show was the longest-running one-person show in New York history. And Horne's career was not over: there were to be more records and appearances, including at age seventy-seven, a television special for the Arts & Entertainment cable network, a two-day, sold-out concert at Carnegie Hall, and a new jazz album, *We'll Be Together Again*.

Horne's career was based on talent, beauty, and hard work. It was full of paradoxes, just as her childhood swings between her mother and her grandmother had been. As the first black movie star, she was the first black to appear on the cover of a movie magazine. But the only roles Hollywood let her play were demeaning ones. She was a token black, but she wasn't black enough; her skin had to be darkened with special makeup. She led the way for others, but for years she was trapped by the demands of being a role model. She was among the very few blacks who were household names in the first half of this century (including Jesse Owens, Joe Louis, Louis Armstrong, Duke Ellington, Paul Robeson, Marian Anderson, and Rochester), but her scenes were edited out when her movies played in the South. She sang at the Savoy Plaza but couldn't stay overnight there. She married a man as successful as she was, but in the year of their wedding, it was illegal for a black and a white to marry in California; they were married in Paris.

Maybe that's some of what we hear in Horne's singing: an intense love of life and a great bitterness, joy as well as anger, the diamond looks and the panther smile, dazzling, teasing, all silk and sass, elegance and coolness, passion and heat. Fire and ice.

JOHN COLTRANE

J AZZ history could virtually be written around the lives of its saxophonists. No other instrument has two separate categories, alto and tenor (four, if you include the occasional soprano and bass), and none has surpassed the saxophone in occupying the forefront of its genre. By 1960, two of jazz's three most creative saxophonists, Lester Young and Charlie Parker, were dead; the third, Coleman Hawkins, was entering the twilight of his career. Into this gap stepped a fourth luminary who had already been making waves and would continue to do so.

J OHN William Coltrane was born September 23, 1926, in Hamlet, North Carolina; his mother was a church pianist and his father played the violin. As a youngster he learned alto sax and clarinet, and he studied music in Philadelphia, where the family had moved in 1944. After performing with a United States Navy band from 1945–47, Coltrane worked with rhythm-and-blues groups, then spent several months in a band led by hard-toned, swinging alto saxophonist Eddie

Vinson. His first break came with trumpeter Dizzy Gillespie's orchestra in 1949. He stayed with Gillespie for two years and made his first recordings. In 1952–53, he returned to the rhythm-and-blues fold with Earl Bostic's group.

C OOL jazz had been around for years before it became dominant in the progressive movement of the 1950s. As the lighter sides of bebop and mainstream jazz began to find common ground with players like trumpeter Miles Davis and alto saxophonist Johnny Hodges, alliances were formed in

John Coltrane on
an MCA Impulse CD.

various outstanding small groups of the decade. John Coltrane's baptism into cool took place with Hodges in 1953–54; he learned much about phrasing (though less about tone) from Duke Ellington's longtime friend and sideman. In 1955, he made his definitive career move when he joined Davis's quintet. The contrast between Coltrane's large, forthright playing and Davis's introspective style was the key to the quintet's stage appearances and recordings.

Five albums were recorded for Prestige Records before Coltrane left the quintet to enter drug rehabilitation. On some of these he developed chordal changes and other innovations that verged on a revolution in jazz, something that hadn't happened since the early days of bebop more than a decade earlier. Coltrane retuned to perform with pianist Thelonious Monk and recorded with the Red Garland trio. *Blue Trane* (1957) and *Soultrane* (1958) broke new ground altogether, with what one critic called "sheets of sound."

The revolution had arrived! In 1958, John Coltrane rejoined Miles Davis and performed on his landmark albums *Kind of Blue* and *Milestones*, the latter album exploring modal harmonies in jazz. On *My Favorite Things* he introduced a soprano sax on the title track. The following year Coltrane formed his own quartet with pianist McCoy Tyner, bassist Jimmy Garrison and drummer Elvin Jones. They recorded for Impulse, a prestigious new jazz label, and were featured live at the Village Vanguard (with flautist-altoist Eric Dolphy), Birdland, and the Newport Jazz Festival. Coltrane's solos became ever longer and more complex and led to a new form of free jazz that won many fans.

In *A Love Supreme* Coltrane achieved what was called his "spiritual awakening." The music

Coltrane, courtesy of the Frank Driggs Collection.

is based on a four-note phrase, intoned by the quartet at the close of the opening track. The album sold a quarter of a million copies. *Ascension* (1965) reached heights of free improvisation that had only been forecast in earlier albums. His wife, pianist Alice Coltrane, had replaced Tyner in the group and worked closely with Coltrane during this important phase of his life. But it was all too brief, as John Coltrane died of liver cancer on July 17, 1967, in New York. Alice continued to perform his music and supervised the release of many unissued recordings after his death.

THELONIOUS MONK

Thelonious Monk.
Photo courtesy of the
Library of Congress.

INNOVATION has long been the keynote of jazz. Sometimes it stems from insights gained through academic training and sometimes from the desire to overthrow what the artist has come to regard as old or constraining form. With others it may arise from a lack of musical education—working around this void, as Thelonious Monk did, with strange and revolutionary ideas. Either way, innovation happens, though we may appreciate and be more awed by the latter path.

THELONIOUS Sphere Monk was born October 11, 1917, in Rocky Mount, North Carolina. He began playing piano at age eleven, accompanying his mother's singing at a Baptist church in New York, where the family moved during Monk's infancy. His first paid work was at rent parties, and for two years in the late '30s he toured with an evangelical group. His models for the piano were Earl Hines and Art Tatum. In 1940, he joined drummer Kenny Clarke in the house band at Minton's Club, directed by Teddy Hill, in Harlem. Late-hour jam sessions at the uptown house produced some of the most advanced playing ever heard. He performed for a while with Lucky Millinder, then returned to Minton's for the historic sessions with Charlie Parker and Dizzy Gillespie where bebop was born.

I N 1944, Monk recorded with trumpeter Cootie Williams, then with legendary saxophonist Coleman Hawkins on 52nd Street. His first recordings as a leader were made with Art Blakey for Blue Note in 1947. The radical character of his playing continued into the early '50s, well after the shock wave of bebop had subsided; he recorded a few tracks with Sonny Rollins and Max Roach in 1952–54 but was unable to play club dates from 1951–57 because of New York's infamous "cabaret card" law. His career was saved when he signed a long-term contract with Orrin Keepnews of Riverside Records in 1955.

M ONK was a composer of many recorded numbers, including " 'Round About Midnight," "In Walked Bud," "Off Minor," and the early standard,

Thelonius Monk's Straight, No Chaser, the Columbia soundtrack album of a documentary film about Monk. The first words on the album are Monk's: "I'm famous. Ain't that a bitch!"

"Epistrophy," written with Kenny Clarke. Among his Riverside hits was the album *Brilliant Corners*, made with Rollins and Roach. He also recorded with John Coltrane on *Monk's Music* (1957) and with Johnny Griffin on *Misterioso* (1960). From 1962 to 1968, Thelonious Monk recorded a series of less-than-groundbreaking albums for Columbia. After forming a big band in 1959, his main activity during the new decade was leading small groups—mainly his own quartet, featuring tenor saxophonist Charlie Rouse.

M ONK was reunited with Art Blakey in 1971 on two Black Lion albums, *Something in Blue* and *The Man I Love*. He made a world tour with Dizzy Gillespie and saxophonist Sonny Stitt as one of the "Giants of Jazz" in 1971–72, but illness kept him from all but the least strenuous appearances during the period. His last public performance was in 1976, though he joined Gillespie and others at President Carter's White House jazz party in 1978. Thelonious Monk died in Englewood, New Jersey on February 17, 1982. His legacy—individuality in many styles, self-parody, and frequent changes of mood, personal and musical—is one of genius and suffering, two

prime ingredients in the world of
innovation.

Thelonius Monk at the
piano in the 1969
Central Park concert. A Jack
Vartoogian photograph.

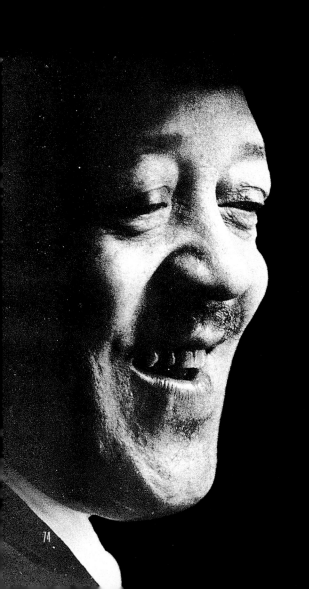

LESTER
YOUNG

MUSICAL soul has been around for a lot longer than its definition of style in the 1950s. In American popular music and jazz, who will say that Louis Armstrong or Billie Holiday didn't possess it—or that tenor saxophonist Lester Young didn't create a world of soul for those around him or for all who followed?

LESTER Willis Young was born in Woodville, Mississippi, on August 27, 1909. He was tutored by his father (who had studied at Tuskegee Institute) in trumpet, alto sax, violin, and drums—an education that proved invaluable as Lester toured the Midwest carnival circuit with the Young family band. They had settled in Minneapolis in 1920, traveling as far as New Mexico and Arizona; it was in Phoenix that Lester, unwilling to tour the South, left the band and moved to Salina, Kansas. There, at the Wiggly Café, he met orchestra leader Art Bronson, who bought him a tenor sax and promptly signed him to tour with his group in January 1928.

Months of working back and forth between the Bronson and the Young family bands landed Lester at the Nest Club in Minneapolis. Early in 1932, he joined the Original Blue Devils, another touring group, before leaving with several members to sign on with Bennie Moten in Kansas City the following year. It was here that Lester Young first performed with Count Basie, joining that musician's legendary breakaway group (with Moten's blessing) in Little Rock, Arkansas. Even in an itinerant field such as jazz, this represented a lot of changes over a very few years; so when Young was offered a permanent job with Fletcher Henderson's orchestra in Detroit, he joined the famous bandleader there on March 31, 1934.

HENDERSON had been a force in music for many years, recording without interruption in his own name (and under a myriad of others) since the middle of 1921. By 1934, a veritable who's who of jazz had played with the orchestra at one time or another: Rex Stewart, Fats Waller, Don Redman, Benny Carter, John Kirby, Russell Procope, Hilton Jefferson, Ben Webster—and the legendary Coleman Hawkins, whom Lester Young replaced in the band. Even this tenure was short-lived, however; after he performed with Henderson in New York, Young's homesickness for the Midwest prevailed, and he left to gig with various bands until settling with Count Basie at the Reno Club in Kansas City during 1936.

BY this time, Young's playing had settled into the smooth, vibratoless style for which he was to become famous. Lightness, clarity, and understatement were his trademarks, elements which—following Hawkins's blunt, foreground-type playing—hadn't been appreciated in Fletcher Henderson's jazz format. Equally original were Young's flights of melodic fancy, excursions that would make him the most creative improviser between Louis Armstrong and Charlie Parker. From the first small-group session with Basie in Chicago, through the big-band dates for Decca that began on January 21, 1937,

Young's definitive tenor sax blazed new trails in jazz.

THE tenure with Basie lasted, perhaps surprisingly, for nearly four years. It was a time of recovery for the U.S. economy and for the record industry in particular, which (from the double causes of radio and the Great Depression) had sunk to a disastrous low after the crash of 1929. Music led the way for the country's new optimism, and nowhere was this feeling of freedom expressed more eloquently than in jazz.

AT the same time he was playing with Basie, Young began recording with the small band of Teddy Wilson—the famous pianist in Benny Goodman's quartet—whose ensemble included Goodman himself, trumpeter Roy Eldridge, bassist John Kirby, drummer Cozy Cole—and the incomparable vocals of Billie Holiday. Recording with Wilson in 1937, Lester Young alternated on tenor sax with Ben Webster and Vido Musso (of later Stan Kenton fame), pairing also with alto sax great Johnny Hodges. The real collaboration, however, was with Holiday. Selections from January 25—such as "I Must Have That Man," "Why Was I Born?" "This Year's Kisses," and Irving Berlin's little-known "He Ain't Got Rhythm"—have been called the epitome of jazz for the period. On May 11 and June 1, they all returned to the Brunswick studio in New York for more great, largely improvised performances—including "I'll Get By" and "Mean to Me"—that made recording history. This also marked the beginning of Lester Young's affair with Billie Holiday, during which she nicknamed him "the president," or just simply Prez.

YOUNG left the Basie band in 1940, worked with a combo briefly at Kelly's Stables in New York, then joined his drummer brother Lee with the Esquires of Rhythm in Los Angeles for the years 1941–43. After a brief return to Count Basie, Young worked a USO tour with Al Sears, rejoined Basie at the Apollo and played with Dizzy Gillespie at the Onyx Club, both in New York, and then went back to Basie from December 1943 to September 1944 before being inducted into the U.S. Army at Fort MacArthur the following month. His army career was a disaster: during combat training he was hospitalized, then court-martialed and imprisoned for using marijuana.

ALTHOUGH he led various small groups and toured annually with Norman Granz's Jazz at the Philharmonic, Lester Young never regained his premilitary level of perfect phrasing and tone. Bebop and the Jazz at the

Philharmonic performing styles were less introverted and refined, while the mainstream saxophonists who did emulate him were energetic and committed, and increasingly numerous as the years went by.

THE high points of his later career were a Carnegie Hall concert with his own group on February 21, 1951, a recording of "There Will Never Be Another You" in 1952, an overseas tour called Birdland 1956, and a Jazz Giants album with his mentor and leader of twenty years before, Teddy Wilson. His last series of appearances (he was hospitalized in '56, '57, and '58) was at the Blue Note Club in Paris, where he collapsed with stomach problems. Lester Young died within twenty-four hours of his return to the United States, on March 15, 1959. He is buried at Evergreen Cemetery in Queens, New York.

Count Basie (top) with
Lester Young, 1944.
Courtesy of the
Frank Driggs Collection.

77

COLE
MAN
HAW
KINS

STRENGTH and adaptability are important in any profession. Having both implies that a person can "go with the flow" while keeping his integrity—that thing at his core—intact. In jazz, as elsewhere, this combination exists all too rarely: more often there is either a blurring of boundaries or, lamentably, becoming stuck in a rut. One artist who transcended both pitfalls, keeping it all together and flourishing, was the great tenor saxophonist Coleman Hawkins. Born on November 21, 1901, in St. Joseph, Missouri, Hawkins bore witness to six decades of jazz—seeing more changes, innovations, and reversions to style than a Paris fashion house—and remained his own person as man and performer through it all.

HE studied piano and cello as a child, taking up the tenor sax at the tender age of nine. By eleven he was performing with school bands, and at sixteen he was playing professionally around the Kansas City area. While performing in a theater orchestra, he was heard by singer Mamie Smith;

in the summer of 1921 (the year after she recorded "Crazy Blues," the first authentic solo blues disc), Hawkins was invited to join her touring group, the Jazz Hounds. He played with them until 1923, when he left for New York.

WHAT followed was the break of a lifetime: after freelancing in New York for a year, Hawkins signed on with Fletcher Henderson and his orchestra. In the fields of recording, touring, theaters, and club dates, where such white bands as those led by Paul Whiteman, Jean Goldkette, and Ben Pollack received prime bookings, Henderson was proving at least their equal in skill and style. His band also rivaled theirs as a seedbed for budding jazz greats. Coleman Hawkins stayed with Fletcher Henderson for ten years, until early 1934, playing with the likes of Louis Armstrong, Rex Stewart, Don Redman, John Kirby, Dicky Wells, and Benny Carter. From Armstrong, Hawkins learned new, flexible, sometimes vocal phrasings on the tenor sax, making his instrument crucial to jazz and himself the most versatile

Body and Soul, the first Vintage album, an RCA reissue, featuring Coleman Hawkins.

saxophonist of his generation.

FOR the next five years, Coleman Hawkins worked overseas—with Jack Hylton's famous orchestra in England and the Ramblers in Holland, among others. He performed on the Continent with the great jazz guitarist Django Reinhardt and fellow expatriates such as Henderson alumnus Benny Carter. When he returned to the United States in 1939, Hawkins found new trends flourishing in postdepression New York: cool, swinging jazz soloists abounded, some of whom, having learned from him, played with incredible speed and facility. But no one had replaced him, and this fact was celebrated that fall with Hawkins's landmark RCA Bluebird recording of "Body and Soul," a heart-stopping performance now in the National Academy of Recording Arts and Sciences Hall of Fame.

Hawkin's recording band, which performed at Kelly's Stables in New York, paved the way for the formation of a big band that opened at the Arcadia Ballroom in November 1939. They also played at the Apollo Theater and the Savoy and Golden Gate ballrooms in New York before disbanding in 1941. After that time, Hawkins led smaller groups, touring the United States and eventually landing in Los Angeles, where he opened Billy Berg's club in 1945. Bebop was now the rage in jazz,

and while Coleman Hawkins often played with the best of them—in Jazz at the Philharmonic concerts, notably—he kept intact the deep-toned, vibrato-based style he had always displayed.

In May 1948, Hawkins returned to Europe for appearances at the Paris Jazz Festival, which he revisited in 1949 and 1950. During the 1950s, he led and sat in with various small groups, mainly in New York, including a mainstream quintet with Roy Eldridge.

Hawkins made a highly acclaimed album, *The High and Mighty Hawk*, in 1957, produced by English-born jazz writer Stanley Dance for the Felsted label. During the 1960s, Coleman Hawkins was heard at such leading New York jazz spots as the Metropole and the Village Gate. He recorded with Duke Ellington in 1962, and a year later released *Today and Now*, an album for the Prestige label that showed his many strengths. Hawkins toured Britain as a soloist in November 1967 and appeared with Eldridge on a

Chicago television show early in 1969.

As one might expect, Hawkins was active until the end, performing only weeks before his death in New York on May 19, 1969. Few have left such a legacy of music making and influence over so extended a period. The description "Jazz Legend" was never better applied to anyone.

GERRY MULLIGAN

Gerry Mulligan at the 1973 Newport Jazz Festival in New York City. Photograph © Jack Vartoogian.

Gerry Mulligan, born in 1927 in New York, came up through the ranks, writing arrangements for radio musicians, touring with the Tommy Tucker band, and working as a sideman with the Gene Krupa band in 1946 and 1947. Some of his first kudos came for his work as a composer/arranger. His "Disc Jockey Jump" was recorded by Krupa's band in 1947. His arrangement of the bop anthem "How High the Moon" was also recorded by Krupa. Emerging as a top name on recordings with Miles Davis from 1948 through 1950, he later was one of the featured soloists in the Stan Kenton orchestra.

THE Davis band grew out of a series of playing sessions at Gil Evans's apartment. Evans was then the chief arranger for pianist Claude Thornhill's band—a big bebop group for which Mulligan had also done some arranging, and in which he had temporarily played saxophone. Evans and Davis had also worked together, and their musical thinking was evolving in similar ways.

THE three musicians—Miles Davis, Gil Evans, and Gerry Mulligan—began thinking about forming a new group, talking about how it should sound and what its instrumentation should be. Evans and Mulligan added French horn and a tuba to the prevailing instrumentation of the modern jazz ensemble, and their scoring produced a new, light sonority. Their new sound featured more melody instruments than the traditional bop combo

Gerry Mulligan's *Two of a Mind*, an RCA album.

and no homogenous orchestra sections the way the big bands did. There was one of each instrument: trumpet, trombone, French horn, and tuba for the brass; baritone and alto sax; a piano, bass, and drums for rhythm. (At various times the group featured, in addition to Miles and Mulligan, Kai Winding or J. J. Johnson on trombone, Junior Collins on French horn, John Barber on tuba, Lee Konitz on alto sax, Al Haig or John Lewis on piano, Joe Shulman on bass, and Max Roach or Kenny Clarke on drums.) Davis called their music "a collaborative experiment."

The new group was booked

into the Royal Roost, and the sign outside said, "Miles Davis's Nonet; Arrangements by Gerry Mulligan, Gil Evans, and John Lewis." Davis said later that he had to fight with the owner of the Roost to get the Nonet in—he wasn't happy about paying for nine musicians when he usually only had to pay for five. The resultant recordings, featuring a mellow Miles Davis lead like the one on "Boplicity" and "Birth of the Cool," sent the new sound around the world.

HERE was a casual grace, deliberately achieved—a pleasant, cool blend radically different from the traditional big-band sound of the thirties and forties. Bop was a conscious revolt against swing; cool jazz evolved out of bop. Gerry Mulligan's later music, after he moved to California in 1952, was labeled "West Coast Jazz," and that was a tributary of cool.

Mulligan broke fresh ground with his California quartet. It included a trumpet, baritone sax, string bass, and drums. No piano, no guitar—a first. The resulting sound of the Gerry Mulligan Quartet, with Chet Baker on trumpet, was a new emphasis on melody and rhythm over harmonics. This is not to say that harmonics were forgotten by the quartet, but without the piano's explicit chord changes, they were implied rather than overt. The melody has more room to stretch, and the texture is lean and clear. Mulligan's recording of "Makin' Whoopee" is a prime example of the new sound. It required great ensemble playing from each of the quartet's members, and the complex, interwoven playing of Mulligan and Baker achieved enormous popularity.

AFTER recording with Lee Konitz and writing arrangements for Stan Kenton, Mulligan formed his second quartet with Bob Brookmeyer on trombone, Red Mitchell on bass, and Frank Isola on drums. By now Mulligan was one of the most popular mainstream jazz leaders of the day. He appeared in the films *I Want to Live* and *The Subterraneans*, and his group was featured in *Jazz on a Summer's Day*, a film about the Newport Jazz Festival.

MULLIGAN took his first European tour with a thirteen-piece band in 1960; in 1964, he toured Japan. He has appeared at dozens of jazz festivals, with Dixie, swing, and bop groups. He is a twenty-time winner of the annual *Down Beat* poll as top baritone sax. Gerry Mulligan is an easy performer, the goodwill ambassador of jazz. He has great rapport with audiences—who may or may not remember that he played a vital part in the evolution of modern jazz.

Gerry Mulligan in 1994.
Photograph © Pamela Stanfield.

STAN GETZ

"THE Sound": that's what they called Stan Getz, often credited as the musician responsible for the first full emergence of the modern tenor saxophone. With Lennie Tristano and Miles Davis, he was among the most important instrumentalists in the creation of the sound known as cool. He was, in the years of his prime, the polished center of cool jazz.

BORN in Philadelphia in 1927, Getz grew up in the Bronx. Playing the bass fiddle in junior high school, he switched to the bassoon in high school to get into the main orchestra. Next, he learned the harmonica. Somewhere along the line Getz picked up tenor sax. He was chosen for the All-City Orchestra, made up of New York City's best high-school musicians. And then, when he was fifteen, he dropped out of school. Joining Dick Rogers's band, he was picked up by a truant officer and put back in school, dropped out again, and teamed up with Jack Teagarden. Teagarden signed guardianship papers for Getz, and that kept him out of school.

Stan Getz at the Newport Jazz Festival in 1966. Courtesy of the Frank Driggs Collection.

THE job with Teagarden went from coast to coast, leaving Getz in Los Angeles. He worked a series of short-term jobs, played the last fifteen broadcasts of the *Bob Hope Show* with Stan Kenton, joined Jimmy Dorsey for a month, and then signed on with Benny Goodman for half a year. This strange progression thus went from Dixie (Teagarden) to progressive jazz (Kenton) back to big-band swing (Goodman). But not all the way. Getz carried Charlie Parker and Lester Young records with him on the road and practiced playing bepop ("in the closet, very secretly") with band members like Kai Winding. Getz was only about seventeen years old, but his talent was already outstanding. He can be heard on the Benny Goodman recordings of "Swing Angel," "Give Me the Simple Life," and "Rattle and Roll," and on the small band sides he made with Winding.

Another series of short jobs followed, the last in a group that called itself the Four Brothers—Getz, Herb Steward, Jimmy Giuffre, and Zoot Sims, with Beverly Byrne—Mrs. Getz, on vocals. They joined Woody Herman's Second Herd as a group in 1947. The cool sound of Getz's saxophone solos on the Herd recording of "Early Autumn" captured the imagination of many jazz saxophonists. After that record there were two jazz-saxophone camps: the hard bop style of Coleman Hawkins and Charlie Parker; and the limpid, soft, airy sound, dazzling bop virtuosity, and the long melodic flow of Stan Getz.

TWO years later Getz was leading his own groups. After touring Europe with Jazz at the Philharmonic in 1958, he remained abroad for three years, settling in Denmark. He kept playing, doing dates and concerts in Scandinavia and Western Europe. When he returned to the States in 1961, John Coltrane had emerged as the tenor saxophonist of note—calling himself "the best of the angry tenors."

But a year later, Getz reemerged at the top with an album called *Focus*, featuring the writing of Eddie Sauter, with Getz

85

improvising over music for strings. The *Down Beat* review called it a magnificent work, "not quite like anything ever before attempted." The album, said the review, was well balanced and ambitiously planned, without losing "the spontaneity, lift, and inventiveness of good jazz playing. . . . Getz plays like an angel."

THE biggest Stan Getz hits—the music that will undoubtedly keep his name always at the top of the list of jazz legends—grew out of his collaboration with guitarist Charlie Byrd in the early sixties. Byrd was talking about the music he'd heard during a tour of Brazil and suggested they do some of the songs together. In 1962, at the All Souls Unitarian Church in Washington, D.C., the two got together to record the album, *Jazz Samba*. On it were two tunes composed by Antonio Carlos Jobim: "Desafinado" ("Slightly Out of Tune") and "Samba de una Nota So" ("One Note Samba"). It launched the beginning of the American bossa nova craze, and the album became one of the biggest sellers in jazz history.

THE words "bossa nova" weren't used in the album title or on the liner notes—they are the Brazilian phrase for "new wrinkle" or "new wave," and they are forever after linked with the melodic and sensuous alliance between jazz and the samba beat. It was a perfect musical marriage, and the groom was Stan Getz. Bossa nova swept the country— dozens of jazz, pop, and Latin artists jumped on its bandwagon. Getz made two more splendid albums, *Big Band Bossa Nova* and *Jazz Samba Encore*, in 1962 and 1963.

IN his next recording, he planned to use the voice and guitar of João Gilberto, Brazil's well-known and very talented bossa nova singer, as well as the piano of Jobim. But Gilberto only sang in Portuguese, so, almost as an afterthought, Getz asked Astrud Gilberto, Jobim's wife, to do a couple of numbers in English. Their version of "The Girl from Ipanema" became an instant hit—it sold over twenty-seven million copies around the world.

Getz won Grammy Awards for both "Desafinado" (1962) and "The Girl from Ipanema" (1964), the latter as record of the year. It was also voted the best jazz performance of 1964.

THERE was more work to follow: more bossa nova; an album featuring the compositions of Eddie Sauter, David Raksin, and Alec Wilder for tenor sax and orchestra, played by Getz and the Boston Pops Orchestra under Arthur Fiedler; a movie sound track; and music making around the world. Getz died on June 6, 1991, with an exciting and versatile career in jazz as his legacy.

Stan Getz Appearing at Tanglewood With Arthur Fiedler and the Boston Pops Orchestra, an RCA album, 1967.

MODERN JAZZ QUARTET

T HE Modern Jazz Quartet was
founded in 1952 by pianist
John Lewis, vibraphonist Milt
Jackson, bassist Percy Heath,
and drummer Kenny Clarke.
Their purpose was avowedly
experimental—to apply classical
music discipline and form to jazz,
creating a new genre that, it was
hoped, would appeal to listeners
of both musical
styles. It was also
a conservative
reaction to the
exuberance and
dissonance of
bebop, in which
each quartet
player had roots
and years of
involvement.
Whatever its
goals, the MJQ
was enormously successful, stay-
ing together (except for the substi-
tution of drummer Connie Kay in
1954) for over two decades as a
jazz force, viable and influential to
countless soloists and groups that
followed.

John Aaron Lewis was born
May 3, 1920, in La Grange,

The Modern Jazz
Quartet.
Photograph ©
Richard Dunkley.

The Modern Jazz Quartet on an Atlantic album. Percy Heath is on the bass (lower left), John Lewis is on piano (upper left), Milt Jackson is on vibraharp (upper right), and Connie Kay is on drums (lower right).

Illinois. He grew up in Albuquerque and studied anthropology at the University of New Mexico before serving in the military in World War II. After his discharge, Lewis entered the Manhattan School of Music and became active on the New York scene, performing with progressive musicians such as Kenny Clarke, who encouraged him to join Dizzy Gillespie's big band in 1945 as pianist-arranger. His scores for Gillespie included such bebop standards as "Emanon,"

"Two Bass Hit," and "Minor Walk." While playing with Illinois Jacquet in 1948, Lewis continued to write for Gillespie and was largely responsible for Miles Davis's chamber jazz project of 1949–50.

I N the early 1950s, John Lewis freelanced with Gillespie, tenor saxophonist Lester Young, and others, perfecting his austere keyboard style and finding ways to incorporate this into small-group formats. Even after the Modern Jazz Quartet was off and running, Lewis experimented on his own: the large-orchestra *European Windows* album, made for RCA Victor in 1958, is a "classical" example. His film scores included *No Sun in Venice* (1957), *Odds Against Tomorrow* (1959), and *A Milanese Story* (1962). Although the MJQ officially closed shop in 1974, John Lewis has made periodic comebacks with them since 1982.

M ILTON Jackson was born in Detroit on January 1, 1923. He attended Michigan State University, then began gigging with bands in the Detroit area

during the early 1940s. In New York, Jackson became bebop's first vibraphone player, joining Dizzy Gillespie's big band in 1946 and later performing with pianists Thelonious Monk, Tadd Dameron, and John Lewis, and with Detroit trumpeter Howard McGhee—progressive musicians all. In 1951, he formed the Milt Jackson Quartet with Lewis, Percy Heath, and Kenny Clarke. When signed to record for Prestige Records the following year, the group came to be called the Modern Jazz Quartet.

M UCH of the group's longevity and strength derived from the tension between Lewis's precise, almost classical, piano and Jackson's free-form, bluesy vibraphone. Listening to "Emanon," recorded by the Gillespie band in 1946, one hears this contrast in its early stages— Lewis's cool, unadorned introduction and Jackson's many-noted, chromatic solo that follows. It was the collaboration of brilliant attempts to bridge this stylistic gap that made the MJQ's performances so fascinating. By and large, the Lewis approach prevailed—a fact that led to Clarke's departure—giving the group top musical material for over two decades.

KENNETH Spearman Clarke was born January 9, 1914, in Pittsburgh, Pennsylvania. His earliest performing years were spent with Leroy Bradley's band, before joining Roy Eldridge in 1935. It was with Teddy Hill's orchestra in 1939–40 that Clarke became the key drummer in the movement leading to bebop. Hill conducted at Minton's Club in Harlem where Clarke—along with Charlie Parker, Dizzy Gillespie, Thelonious Monk, and others— was integral to the movement's sound and style. Departing from the steady four-beat rhythms of mainstream jazz, Clarke introduced unexpected off-beats and wild variations that raised the sta-

The Modern Jazz Quartet in 1975.
Courtesy of the Frank Driggs Collection.

tus of drumming in jazz and made it far more interesting.

AFTER leaving the Modern Jazz Quartet, Kenny Clarke worked mainly in France, playing at the Blue Note club between 1961–67. He formed the Clarke-Boland big band with pianist Francy Boland in 1960; it lasted until 1973, almost as long as the MJQ. His extensive discography runs from early RCA Victor sides with Sidney Bechet to Dizzy Gillespie's DeeGee label in the '50s to Clarke-Boland albums on Atlantic and Prestige in the '60s

and '70s. After 1973, he appeared with various small groups in Europe, returning occasionally to the United States for reunion performances. He died in Paris on January 25, 1985.

PERCY Heath was born April 30, 1923, in Wilmington, North Carolina, and grew up in Philadelphia. After military service he played locally for two years, then joined Howard McGhee's combo in 1947, during New York's bebop heyday. He appeared with bop trumpeters Fats Navarro and Miles Davis, then joined Dizzy Gillespie's band from 1950–52. When Milt Jackson formed his own quartet the following year, Heath was the regular bassist, and the rest is MJQ history. His elegant playing contributed much to the group's image of cool musical restraint.

The double album *European Concert* (1960) and the *Porgy and Bess* album (1964) were high points in the group's career. *Last Concert* (1974) was their recorded swan song.

The Modern Jazz Quartet, Left to Right: John Lewis, Connie Kay, Percy Heath, Milt Jackson.

AFTER the Modern Jazz Quartet's dissolution, its members went in different directions. John Lewis returned to academe, teaching jazz courses and performing on occasion. Milt Jackson appeared on numerous live sessions for the Pablo label of Norman (Jazz at the Philharmonic) Granz. Connie Kay has performed with Dixieland bands in the United States, while Percy Heath formed a jazz-funk trio with brothers Jimmy (alto sax) and Albert (drums). The Heath Brothers have recorded for Columbia. The MJQ was reunited at the Newport Jazz Festival in 1981 and cut a Duke Ellington tribute compact disc for East-West in 1988 with substitute personnel. Theirs is a musical story without end.

92

AFTERWORD

We don't think about people not being here. If we think about Lester Young, we don't think, well, Lester Young was here but he's not here anymore. Lester Young is here. Coleman Hawkins is here. Roy Eldridge is here. They are in us, and they will always be alive.

Art Farmer,
A Great Day in Harlem

I won't be thinking about Jimmy being dead, because my head doesn't work that way. I'll miss them, but Gil is still in my head, like Jimmy is, like Trane and Bud and Monk and Bird and Mingus and Red and Paul....All my best friends are dead. But I can hear them.

Miles Davis,
The Autobiography

A Note From the Authors About the Organization of This Book:

We considered several possible ways of organizing the profiles in this book—alphabetically, chronologically, or in a way which would combine the progression of time with equally clear musical relationships among the performers. The present random order was reached through a technical process over which we had no control. Browse through the names, and as you read, we hope you will find a progression of your own.